Reports & Letters On Light Narrow-Gauge Railways by Sir Charles Fox and Son, M.I.C.E., John Edward Boyd, M.I.C.E., C. Phil, M.I.C.E., Major Adelskold, Swedish Royal Engineer, and Mr. Fitzgibbon, C.E.: With Remarks On the Advantages to Be Derived by the Co

G Laidlaw

PREFACE.

For the purpose of affording the people interested in the construction of the Toronto, Grey and Bruce Railway, and the Toronto and Lake Nipissing Railway, an opportunity of judging of the merits of the Light Narrow Gauge System, upon which these Roads are projected, it has been deemed expedient to explain that the documents following are the statements of eminent Engineers who have built and worked, for a number of years, railroads on the system in question, and that the facts mentioned are not theories, but the valuable results of actual experience.

It was only after an active agitation and discussion of the question for two years, that the Norwegian Parliament finally consented to try the experiment which has given such satisfaction for seven years, that that Government will not now build any other kind of local lines. To Mr. C. Pihl belongs the credit of having inaugurated and put into successful operation this system, which was immediately imitated with equal success and consequent satisfaction by the Government of Queensland (where these roads pay 8 per cent. dividend), and also the Government of India. It is noteworthy that the Governments of Russia and Italy have sent Special Commissions to examine this economical system, with a view to its adoption in these countries, wherever suitable; and there can be no question of the wisdom of adopting in this country a system of Railroads,

within our reach, which will give the people the ines-
timable benefits of Railway accommodation for the
trade of those districts where the more expensive system
is impracticable by reason of its great cost and unprofit-
ableness.   Mr. C. Pihl is, and has been since the adoption of his system of Light Narrow Gauge Railways,
chief engineer to the Government of Norway, and Major
Adelskold is engineer to the Government of Sweden.
The world-known firm of Sir Charles Fox & Sons are
the consulting engineers to the Governments of India
and Queensland, while Mr. Fitzgibbon is the superin-
tending engineer of the Queensland Narrow Gauge
Railways—his cogent remarks on the reasons which led
his Government to adopt this in preference to the old
broad gauge expensive system are well worthy of reflection.

Mr. J. Edward Boyd, C.E., a member of the Institution of Civil Engineers, London, is engineer to the
Government in New Brunswick, and wrote a pamphlet
recommending Light Narrow Gauge Railways in New
Brunswick, in the year 1865, which he sent as a reply
to the questions of the joint Committee on Railways,
appointed by the City Council, the Board of Trade, and
the Corn Exchange.

The writer has no knowledge of engineering, and in
common with his coadjutors, has no other objects to
promote save the advantage of the country, the prosperity of Toronto, and their share of the great increase
of business which will follow the construction of these
necessary works.

                                        G. L.

To the Presidents, Vice-Presidents and
Directors of the Toronto, Grey and Bruce and
Toronto and Nipissing Railway Companies.

GENTLEMEN,—

I have the honour to submit the following information on the Light Railway System of 3 feet 6 inches gauge:

The chief points in question are the cost of construction, the cost of maintenance and the working expenses, the traffic capacity, the speed attainable, and the safety of these narrow gauge lines, as compared with the ordinary lines of 5 feet 6 inches gauge.

It is claimed that a line of 3 feet 6 inches gauge can be built for one-half the cost of a 5 feet 6 inches line constructed in the usual way, and in some districts possibly for less. It may seem strange that the mere reduction of two feet in the gauge can exert so important an influence over the cost of a Railway, but it is, nevertheless, true, and it is believed that any statements here made will bear the fullest investigation.

It will not be disputed that the resistance due to curves and imperfections in the track decreases as the width between the rails is reduced. The greater portion of curve resistance is due to the sliding motion produced by the difference in the space to be passed over by two wheels of equal diameter keyed fast to opposite ends of an axle common to both. Inequalities in the surface give the wheels a tendency to bind diagonally across the track. It can easily be understood, therefore, that both these resistances diminish with the length of the axle—or what is the same thing, the width of the gauge. It is by taking advantage of this ability which the narrow gauge lines possess of adapting themselves to the natural surface of the country by sharper or more frequent curves without the result of a corresponding loss of power from increased resistance, that a great part of the saving in earthwork is effected. The remainder is due to the decreased width of the cuttings and embankments (see figs. 1, 2 and 3). The saving in earthwork naturally leads to a saving in masonry—if the embankments are narrower and lower, the culverts are shorter and the bridge abutments of less height and width. As the engines and trains are lighter, the bridge superstructure is much less costly. The comparative cost of one mile of permanent way on the two gauges is as follows:

FIVE FEET SIX INCH LINE.

100 tons Rails at $50 per ton	$5,000	0
Fish Plates, Bolts and Spikes	800	0
Sleepers, 2,263	700	0
Ballast, 3,000 cubic yards	1,200	0
Tracklaying	400	0
	8,100	0

THREE FEET SIX INCH LINE.

60 tons Rails at $50 per ton	$3,000	0
Fish Plates, Bolts and Spikes	400	0
Sleepers, 2,263	500	0
Ballast, 2,250 cubic yards	900	0
Tracklaying	300	0
	5,100	0

In Queensland, 200 miles of 3 feet 6 inch lines are now being worked, and some 250 miles more are in progress. Mr. Fitzgibbon, the chief engineer to the Government, says in his report: "It was found on a calculation of the " quantities of work, that the cost of the line with 4 feet 8½ " inch gauge would exceed that of the 3 feet 6 inch gauge ", by more than threefold." This is, it is true, an extreme case, because the country was exceedingly difficult; but on the other hand, it must be remembered that the comparison is between the 3 feet 6 inch gauge and the 4 feet 8½ inch, not the 5 feet 6 inch. Major Adelskold, Swedish Royal Engineers, who has constructed several of these Railways, says: "Their principal advantage is their " original cost, which is so considerably below that of the " broader (4 feet 8½ inch) gauge both here and in Norway." The Editor of "The Engineer," commenting on his report, says: "We are indebted to Major Adelskold for " his valuable information on the Swedish Railway System, " and agree with his views of the economical advantages of " the narrow gauge system. After the experience gained, " we think it may be safely stated that the cost of a Rail- " way diminishes in proportion with the gauge." M. Carl Pihl, chief engineer of the Norwegian Government Railways, says: "The formation width for the line of 4 feet " 8½ inch gauge is generally from 15 feet to 18 feet, say 16½ " feet on an average; and for the 3 feet 6 inch gauge, it is " here 12 feet 6 inches. The average height of the banks and " cuttings on the narrower gauge is less than on the broad, " owing to the greater facility of adaptation to the country. " With us the height is 10 feet, whereas had the broader " gauge been adopted it would have been 12 feet to 14 " feet, say 13 feet. This would make the proportion of " quantities nearly as 4 to 7." (See fig. 3.)

Sir Charles Fox and Son, speaking of such a line in this country, says: "We have appended an estimate of the " cost, in which we believe we have fully provided for con- " tingencies, and which amounts to £3000 per mile."

Mr. Frank Shanly estimates the cost of a light 5 feet 6 inch line on your route, fully equipped and including right

of way and fencing, at $15,400 per mile; but he says else-
where that the first cost of such a line would exceed that
of a 3 feet 6 inch line by from 5 to 10 per cent.; the deduc-
tion of 5 per cent. (Sir Charles Fox estimates the difference
at 30 per cent.) would make the cost $14,630 per mile.
Mr. Shanly's professional standing and his knowledge of
the district prevent any doubts as to the reliability of this
estimate, and I must, therefore, be safe in estimating the
probable cost of your Railway at $15,000 per mile.

I wish particularly to impress upon you that none of the
advocates of the Light Narrow Gauge Railways propose to
arrive at this saving in first cost by inferior construction
or the use of inferior materials, and I would be the last to
advise such false economy. The object is to construct
lines which, though their first cost be low, will not be
expensive to work and maintain. And in order to meet
these two important requirements, it is neccessary that the
materials and workmanship should be of the very best
description, and properly proportioned to the services they
have to perform.

Of the Queensland lines, Mr. Fitzgibbon says: "As
"regards the quality and durability of the works, of the
"rolling stock and the equipment of the line, nothing is
"left to be desired;" and again: "the construction of the
"road and the various appliances employed are in all
"respects equal to any Railway in the world [excepting
"only that they are limited in power to the wants of the
"case." Sir Charles Fox and Son, the consulting engineers
to the Queensland Government, say: "The principle
"adopted on these lines is to make them in the very best
"manner, and to spare no necessary expense to ensure
"materials and workmanship of first-class quality. The
"rolling stock is of the very best description, and the pas-
"senger carriages quite equal for comfort to the best in
"this country." Mr. Charles Douglas Fox says of the
Norwegian lines, of which he made a thorough examina-

tion: "I would again testify to the excellent condition
"of all the works on the lines; the permanent way, some of
"which has stood the test of two Norwegian winters, is,
"without exception, the smoothest road I have been on."

The cost of maintenance of the narrow-gauge must be
less than that of the broad, if only for the reason that the
perishable parts are less expensive to replace.

Major Adelskold says : "The working expenses have
"also been considerably lower, partly because the resist-
"ance on the curves with the same speed diminishes in
"proportion with the gauge; partly, also, because the dead
"weight of the carriages comparatively diminishes with
"the gauge; and finally, because the light locomotives on
"a narrow-gauge line do not wear out the rails so easily as
"a heavier engine on a broader gauge."

Mr. Robert Mallet, Mem. Inst. C. E., at the discussion of this question before the Institution, said :—"That
"in proportion as the gauge was reduced, both the first
"cost and working expenses would be diminished." My
own impression is, that while the cost of repairs would
be less per mile, the actual expense of moving a passenger
or a ton of goods would be about the same per mile on
either gauge, and this seems to be Sir Charles Fox's view
when he says that these Railways "will, under proper
"management, be worked and maintained at at least as
"low a percentage as ordinary lines."

It is somewhat difficult to estimate the full traffic capacity of a prospective Railway. The London and North
Western of England, with a double track of 4 feet 8½ inch
gauge, carries 20,000,000 of passengers per annum, and
has the largest freight traffic in England, and probably in
the world. Its revenue is nearly £2,000,000 per annum,
more than twice the revenue of the Great Western, with its
double track of 7 feet gauge. The Grand Trunk, 5 feet 6
inch gauge, carried, in half year ending 31st December,
1866, 792,487 passengers and 523,865 tons of freight, equal

to say 1,600,000 passengers, and 1,100,000 tons of goods per annum; but the New York Central, 4 feet 8½ inch gauge, single line, below Syracuse, carried 3,740,156 passengers, and 1,602,197 tons of freight.

Mr. Fitzgibbon estimates the capacity of the Queensland Railway at 400 tons of goods and 800 passengers per day of 12 hours, equal in all to about 146,067 tons per annum, and adds: "By running night trains, this estimate may "be doubled, and by laying down a second line of rails, it "may be increased six-fold." Major Adelskold estimates the capacity of one of the Swedish lines at 100,000 passengers, and 150,000 tons of goods, equal to about 158,333 tons per annum. In the first of these estimates allowance must be made for the steep gradients of 1 in 50, some of which are of great length, combined with sharp curves on the Queensland lines, and in the second, for the limited supply of rolling stock on which the estimate is based. Both these estimates are therefore within the mark, for Sir Charles Fox says the locomotives are capable of drawing with ease trains weighing 150 tons gross, equal to about 85 tons net, up gradients of 1 in a 100, with curves of 330 feet radius, at a speed of 20 miles per hour; and assuming this as a basis, 6 trains per day would carry 160,000 tons per annum, and there would be no difficulty in having double that number of trains if necessary.

Mr. F. Shanly's estimate of the probable traffic to be drawn from the district through which your line will pass is 300 tons freight, and 200 passengers per day, which would only require four trains. M. Pihl says of the Norwegian lines: "Should that fortunate time arrive when the "traffic has developed to such an extent that the line as "originally constructed proves insufficient, then I believe "that a double line would naturally suggest itself as meet-"ing the requirements of increased traffic every way bet-"ter than a single line of wide gauge. The cost of the ad-"dition would, based upon calculations made for the pur-

" pose, be rather more than 50 per cent. of the original
" cost of the line proper, stations and rolling stock not
" included, and the total of this double line would then
" cost about the same as the single 4 feet 8½ in. would
" originally have cost," and consequently less than a single
5 feet 6 inch line would originally have cost. It is clear
that with this facility of adding at any time to the capacity,
it is bad policy to expend twice the amount required for
present purposes, merely to meet a want which may not
be felt for thirty years, and is simply to expend, in interest
alone, a large sum which would be much better employed
in extending Railways into other districts. The traffic on
the Government Railway in Nova Scotia has never exceeded 161,000 passengers and 70,500 tons goods per annum, and in New Brunswick, 149,000 passengers, and, 55,500
tons goods, so that a line of 3 feet 6 inch gauge would so far
have accommodated all their traffic quite as well as the
present 5 feet 6 inch lines.

The present tendency is everywhere towards a reduction,
rather than an increase in the gauge of Railways. The
Great Western Railway Company of England have laid
down a third rail to the 4 feet 8½ inch gauge on their
7 feet line, and it is their intention, as the broad gauge
rolling stock wears out, to replace it with that adapted to the
narrow gauge.

As the centre of gravity is lowered, and the engines and
cars are constructed with an angle of stability which is nearly
the same on either gauge, the absolute safety must be quite
as great on the 3 feet 6 inch lines as on the 4 feet 8½ inch,
or the 5 feet 6 inch lines. (See diagrams.) The ordinary
speed of express trains in Canada and the United States is
from 25 to 30 miles per hour, including stoppages, and
mixed and freight trains are not, or should not be, run faster
than from 15 to 20 miles per hour.

It is found from actual experience that the Queensland
Railways, already in operation, are perfectly capable of

conducting goods and passenger traffic at an average rate of from 20 to 30 miles per hour, including stoppages, with ease and safety. "On the Swedish lines the general " speed for mixed trains is 16 miles per hour, but it has " on several occasions been brought up to from thirty to " thirty-five miles, when both carriages and waggons moved " with perfect steadiness." Mr. C. D. Fox, in his report on the Norwegian Railways, says, "The train on which I " was, consisted of six carriages and a brake-van, and we " ran with great ease and perfect steadiness, at the rate of " thirty-two miles per hour; the ordinary working speed " does not, however, exceed 15 miles per hour, including " stoppages. The line is kept in a most creditable state " of repair, not surpassed by any English railway, and my " impression certainly is, that the running of the trains is " particularly free from any vibration."

Speaking of another line, he says, "the train with which " I came consisted of six goods waggons full, one empty, " one cattle waggon full, four passenger carriages nearly " full, and the brake-van, or an aggregate gross load of 118 " tons, which we ran with at sometimes thirty miles per hour, " with perfect ease; nothing can exceed the steadiness of " both engines and carriages."

Mr. Pihl, in a letter to the editor of *Engineering*, 7th of March, 1867, says, "The regular trains are run here at " 14 miles an hour, including stoppages, or 16 to 20 miles " between stations, the very same speed at which the " mixed trains run on the 4 feet 8½ inch gauge here. As to " the safety of fast running, engines and carriages appear " to run as safely and steadily at 30 miles an hour on the " 3 feet 6 inch gauge, as they do on one of 4 feet 8½ inch, " and I have run the very engine illustrated in your jour- " nal of 21st December last, at upwards of 40 miles an " hour, with as much feeling of ease and security as I have " felt when running any engine on a broader gauge."

Sir Charles Fox says, of the 3 feet 6 inch branch of the

Madras Railway, " The line has now been worked for some " time most satisfactorily, the trains having on several occa- " sions attained a speed of 40 miles an hour, and the working " expenses being moderate."

As the question of adopting a light system of broad gauge lines has been brought up, it may be well to say a few words on them.

Mr. F. Shanly, while he recommends them, says they will cost 5 or 10 per cent. more than the 3 feet 6 inch lines. Sir Charles Fox, in his report to the Madras Railway Company, makes the difference 30 per cent.

Now the weight of rails to be used is the same as on the 3 feet 6 inch lines, the weight of engines is the same, and consequently the adhesion available for traction is the same, and it necessarily follows that the engines cannot possibly draw any heavier load on the light 5 feet 6 inch line than on the 3 feet 6 inch line. Neither Sir Charles Fox nor Mr. Shanly claim that they will draw any more. Indeed, with the same curves and gradients, they could not draw so much, because of the greater curve resistance on the broad gauge. Why then expend 30 per cent., which on a line 100 miles long would amount to $450,000, or even 10 per cent., which would amount to $150,000 more in construction, if you are to get no greater traffic capacity for it, especially as the main argument, the break of gauge, has no weight in the case of your proposed lines ?

There is one other objection urged against the narrow- gauge lines, which a little reflection would show has no sound basis, viz., the inability of the engines to keep the track clear of snow in winter. Fortunately, we have the testimony of experience on this point also. Major Adels- kold says, " Another dislike which I myself entertained " against the narrow gauge, was, that the smaller and " lighter locomotives should not be able to keep the line " open in winter; but experience during several severe

"winters, has shown that with suitably constructed snow
"ploughs, the narrow gauge lines have been kept as free
"from snow as the broader ones."

I have preferred, instead of entering into arguments
based one mere theory, to give the testimony of engineers,
who having constructed and worked lines of 3 feet 6 inch
gauge, can speak from actual experience of their success
in other countries. All the gentlemen whose opinions I
have quoted, are of high professional standing, and hold
positions of responsibility, and they would not express
themselves so decidedly in favour of the light, narrow gauge
system, unless they were fully satisfied of its advantages.

It only remains for me to say that, as far as my knowledge
of the construction and operation of railways enables me
to judge, I feel satisfied that the system would be equally
successful in this country, for all lines except those which
are required to carry a large through traffic at very high
rates of speed.

I have the honor to be, Sir,

Your obedient servant,

JOHN EDW. BOYD,

M. Inst. C. E.

CHRISTIANA, April 13th, 1867.

G. LAIDLAW, ESQ.,
     Toronto, Canada.

SIR,—Your letter of 2nd ult. I received a couple of days
ago, and replying to the same, I shall be most happy to give
you all the information relative to the Railway System of
3 feet 6 inch gauge as adopted in this country, which I think
will be of service to you and to the members of the committee
appointed to consider the important question relative to your
country.

As well as answering a few of the particular questions enumerated in the printed list you enclosed, I will procure you copies of letters sent from here to the Engineers for the Cape Government, one of whom, Mr. E. Guadling, visited Norway last year for the purpose of personal inspection.

The letter from Mr. Schwartz may have an interest. He is a member of our Parliament, and one of our leading men in Railway matters, as well as a director of the Drammen Railway. Mr. Broch, the writer of the other letter, is also a member of Parliament, as well as a managing director for the Hamar Line, and for our lines of the ordinary 4 feet 8½ inch gauge. You will, no doubt, find it interesting to learn that the small traffic of the described line has proved sufficient to pay the working expenses, which is all we have expected before the extension of the line. The next copy is a list, written by myself to Mr. Guadling, and containing data as to construction, cost, etc., of the different lines in work and in course of construction.

I also enclose a few photographs from plans prepared for the Paris Exhibition, and by book-post I send you a copy of an "Exposé" belonging to the plans.

With regard to the much disputed question of gauge, I beg to refer you to an article by me in Mr. Zerah Colburn's paper "Engineering," No. 62, the answer to which you will find No. 63. To this latter I have not yet replied.

Now with regard to your questions:

The Rails.—The weights adopted on our various lines will be seen from the enclosed sections, which we find of sufficient strength [for our engines. The weight on each of the four coupled driving wheels varies from 2¾ to 3 tons on No. 2 and 3, and is 3¼ tons on No. 4. These last rails are made only of puddle bars in place of with hammered slabs for the top and bottom table, as used on Nos. 2 and 3, and I believe this cheaper rail to make also a better and more durable one. The rails are manufactured in South Wales, and the prices have been £7 7s. 6d. in 1858-59, for Nos. 1, 2 and 3, and £7 1s. 6d. in 1865, for Nos. 1 and 4.

I consider the rails ought most unquestionably to be fished, and particularly so those of a small section. I consider chairs needless, and too expensive for cheap and light Railways.

Earthwork.—The saving in earthwork by the introduction of the narrow gauge is all dependent upon the state of the country, and is necessarily more in a hilly and difficult country than in a level one. The width of formation level being limited in proportion to gauge and the maximum weights to move over the same, has been reduced from 18 feet on the 4 feet 8½ inch to 12 feet 6 inch on the narrow gauge. The width I do not think ought for the sake of drainage and repairs to be further reduced, nor do I think, when the construction of the rolling stock is duly considered, a further reduction of gauge advisable or attended with any saving, even if the weight of rails and engines should be reduced to answer a minimum traffic, the rails say to 24 lbs. per yard, and the wheel pressure to 2 tons only.

Bridges—Are here erected all of timber except across rivers where large spans are unavoidable, or ice to hindrance, and where superstructures of iron on stone piers are resorted to. The relative cost between spans of 100 feet of timber and iron is here as 2 to 3. The construction of timber viaducts as per photograph is very simple, cheap, and remarkably rigid even at an elevation of 70 feet and more. We do not preserve the timber except by tarring when fully seasoned and dry.

Grades.—On a railway with small traffic, for which a comparatively small capital can be invested, and where cheap construction is a prime consideration, and a narrow gauge consequently more adaptable than a broad one can and must, also steeper grades be more tolerated than when the reverse is the case.

Curves.—As the resistance in curves increases in direct proportion as the gauge, it follows that with the same length of waggons a proportionally smaller curve can be adopted; or the reverse, larger waggons with same radius of curves.

Cars.—As the gauge has been diminished so has the body of the car been lowered in order to retain nearly the same angle of stability as on the broader gauge. (See photograph.)

The following are particulars of stock:

	Outside.		Weig't	Cargo.	Prices.	
	Width	L'ngth	empty tons.	Net.	3' 6' £	4' 8¼ £
Passenger Carriage 1st and 2nd class,	6' 10	20'	5 9 2	28 pass	230	295
" " 2nd class only.....	6' 10½	20'	4 17 0	30 "	150	258
Brakevan with 1 Camp for passengers	6' 10½	20'	5 10 0	8 " besides lug'age Tons.	170	257
Goods and Timber Waggons..........	6' 10½	{18 24'}	3 3 0	5 0	63	76

Diameter of wheels, 2 feet 6 inches; height to central buffer, 2 feet 6 inches; distance between axles, 10 to 13 feet. All iron-work is made in England; framing here.

The Engines are all "Tank engines" on three pairs of wheels, of which the two pairs are coupled as drivers, and have a diameter of from 3 feet to 3 feet 9 inches. The third axle is fitted either in the common way without side motion, or in movable axle-boxes of the Adams' radial principle, or lastly in front on a "Bissell truck," which last arrangement I prefer. The total weight of charged engines varies from 15 to 17 tons, of which 11 to 13 are made available for traction. The price for each engine, made by the first English manufacturers— Stephenson, Slaughter, Griming & Co., and Beyer, Peacock & Co.—has been from 1,200 to 1,400 pounds, exclusive freight.

Contracts.—*The English system of letting the works as a whole on contract is not used or approved of.* The line is divided in districts of about 7 or 8 miles, each district in charge of a resident engineer, under whom the works are carried out either in small contracts of a few cuttings, and seldom more than a mile or thereabouts, or as piecework by gangs of men with a respectable foreman in charge, who receives a small

2

percentage of the earnings equally divided by all. For instance, the masonry of a large bridge may be let at so much per yard by measurement to one; the superstructure, if of timber, to another; or, if of iron, it is especially contracted for through the office either in England or here, according to circumstances. You will thus see that the works are carried out by ourselves, and having a staff of well-educated and experienced engineers, we find that this system works both well and cheap.

Being entirely unacquainted with the prices of labour and materials in Canada, I can of course give no opinion as to the probable minimum cost with you for a Railway of the class here described, but I will here add, for the guidance for such estimate, the currant [prices of labour here, which are as follows:

A common labourer, 1s. 6d. to 1s. 10d. per day.

A bridge carpenter, 2s. 3d. to 2s. 9d. per day.

A mason, 2s. 3d. to 2s. 9d. per day.

For piecework is paid:

For 1 cubic yard excavation moved into bank, earth, about 6d. in light soil.

For 1 cubic yard excavation moved into rock, average 3s.

Cost of timber equal to labour in erection, or very nearly so, according to class of work.

Lastly, as to the capability of transport on the 3 feet 6 inch gauge Railway, I may state that the engine described, which should move a train of about 420 to 450 tons gross on a level at 14 to 16 miles an hour, moves according to trial about 136 tons up an incline of 1 in 100, at a speed of ten miles an hour.

With regard to the question as to "how little can a railway be built for of 3 feet 6 inch gauge, to carry passengers and cars loaded with 5 tons of freight, at a speed of 16 miles an hour," it is my opinion, as before said, that the width of formation ought not to be less than 12 to 13 feet, as adopted here. The saving has therefore to be sought principally in the size and weight of the engine and the rail. Assuming the rail to be of the similar section as adopted here, then a rail to carry a car of 5 tons net, or 8 tons gross, that is 2 tons on each of 4 wheels, will be one of about 24 lbs. per yard. A locomotive to answer this rail could have a weight of 10 or even 12 tons, of which eight tons available for traction on four coupled driving wheels. In a flat country I have no doubt this would do very well for a small traffic, and this is the very thing I contemplate in order to diminish to a minimum the cost of railways here. This, I think, also would make the cheapest railway with means for a future increase of traffic, when required, by the removal of the present light rails for heavier ones, and the adding of heavier engines also.

The present subject being of great interest to me, I shall feel very pleased if the information here offered can be of service for the matter under consideration, and it would much interest me if you, in time, will favour me with papers, or copies of papers, relating to the subject when discussed.

While writing down this, I have received a few copies of the number of "Engineering" in which is my article above referred to, which I enclose, regretting to have no copy of the next number with the answer at hand, which I trust you can easily get.

Should you desire any further information of which I may be in possession, I shall be most happy to meet your wishes.

I remain, Sir,
Yours obediently,

C. PIHL.

In place of a copy of the list for Mr. Guadling, I have prepared another, and which I think is more suitable for your purpose.

———

The following letters and reports were written to engineers specially engaged by the Government of the Cape, to enquire into the Norwegian system; copies were kindly furnished in the English language to the Provisional Officers of the Toronto, Grey and Bruce, and Nipissing Railway Companies, by Carl Pihl.

G. LAIDLAW, ESQ.,

    Toronto.

DEAR SIR,—Having only a couple of days ago returned, after an absence of some weeks on the continent, I hasten to supply you with the papers lost; but as your letter is not quite clear about which of them are gone, and which are not, I think it best, in order to be safe, to send you copies of them all, hoping they may yet come in time to be of some service to you and the cause.

I at the same time send you a list of comparative cost, amount of work and equipment of our several lines, that I had lately compiled for other purposes, but may have interest also for you. As time, however, is very short for having this despatched by the first mail, I must leave you to reduce the figures to American or English standard, but will merely here state that *one* Norwegian mile is rather better than seven English miles (7.0183), and one specurdaler four shillings and sixpence English.

With the short time left me since my return, I have looked over the papers you kindly sent me, and I find you have the same kind of stubborn opposition and argumentations to face with you as we have had plenty of also here in Europe. Still I am happy to say that, as facts are hard to reduce, the opinions seem now to turn even among people who before were seemingly the last to be convinced. This, I say, is my experience now in England. We have only just now had a visit from the Italian State Engineer, Signor Biglio, who by the order of his Government visited Sweden and Norway, in order to inspect and report upon our Light or Narrow Gauge Railways. I also see now in the papers that the Russian

Government have appointed a Commissioner for the same purpose on account of railways in Finland. This gentleman has to visit Sweden, Norway and Scotland.

In order that you may be able to explain the apparent great difference in expenses in the construction of the line built by my friend Major Adelskold, in Sweden, and those built here by me, I will state that this, from data given me, lies entirely in the quantity of work done, and which is sufficiently apparent from the fact that the Swedish lines, in working order, cost not more than the superstructure (earthwork, rack, &c.) of ours, and this fully illustrates the heavy country and difficulty we have had to clear. I think Mr. Boyd's estimate of $12,000 to $14,000 per mile must, in all probability, be quite enough, as I am of opinion that the difficulties of construction are as much more than ordinary here in Norway, as they have been under it on the Swedish line in question.

My dear sir,

Yours truly,

(Signed,)   C. PIHL

Christiana, July 1, 1867.

CAPE COLONIAL RAILWAY OFFICE, }
32 Charing-cross, London. }

E. GUADLING, ESQ.

SIR,—In reply to your enquiries about the prospects of the Railway system in this country, and, of the influence which the adoption of the 3 feet 6 inch gauge has had, and will probably have, I beg to give you the following particulars.

When our first Railway from Christiana to the lake of Mjosen, was constructed, there arose in several parts of this country a strong desire of possessing a like effective means of communication, and various investigations took place on this subject. The great extent of the country, together with a scanty and spread population (1,700,000 people upon an area of 122,000 English square miles), and the natural obstacles of the highly mountainous country, together with a comparatively small traffic, threatened with making further works of this nature (except the Railway to the frontier, towards Sweden, for communicating with the Swedish Railways) a mere illusion, until Mr. C. Pihl, now the Government Engineer, ventured to propose the adoption of a narrower gauge than the ordinary, say 3 feet 6 inches, English, thereby rendering the expenses of the building to be between half and two-thirds of the former cost. After various considerations, the Government, as well as our Parliament, Storthinget, resolved to adopt Mr. Pihl's plan, and two Railways, one between Hamar and Elverum, the other between Throndhjem and Storen, were built after his plan. The result has not only turned out fully to the satisfaction of the public, but even far exceeds the expectations anticipated, and it has now already for some years been proved that the 3 feet 6 inch gauge Railway, when well constructed and built, affords a sure and effective means of communication both for passengers and goods, even of a comparatively large extent, and that it may be managed at a cheap rate. The result of the adoption of the 3 feet 6 inch gauge has been so satisfactory, that there is at present building—as shown to you—a Railway of the same gauge between the lake of Randstjord and Drammen, about 56 English miles, and calculated for a heavy transport of timber and minerals, as well as a comparatively great number of passengers, and at this moment there is under consideration the construction of other Railways to the extent of about 130 English miles. It is now evident that there will be built Railways with us in various parts of the country, and under circumstances where there could not else have been question of them for series of years, and I also consider it beyond doubt, that Railways of a narrow gauge, like ours, will be the most effective and appropriate means of communication for any country with comparatively limited resources and moderate traffic. The cost of our 3 feet 6 inch Railways has been from £3,200 to £5,000 per English mile, and as a proof of the influence they are supposed to have in the development of the resources of our country, I may mention that the Throndhjem Storen Railway was built, notwithstanding the calculations of the traffic made it probable that it would hardly bear its expenses, and without leaving surplus for interest.

All our Railways, except the Trunk Railway (from Christiana to the lake of Mjosen), have been built by the Government, with contributions from the various corporations or districts, and private individuals.

I am, dear Sir,

Yours most respectfully,

JOH. T. SCHWARTZ,

Director of the Drammen Randsfjord Railway.

Drammen, 28th June, 1866.

———

(Copy.)

CHRISTIANA, Oct. 18, 1886.

E. GUADLING, ESQ.

The Hamar-Elverum Railway has a length of 24 English miles. It leads from Hamar, a country town on the Mjosen lake, with little more than 1000 inhabitants, through and to a very thinly populated district, the Glommen valley, whose principal trade consists in timber traffic. Nevertheless the line is but to a small extent used for transport of the timber, this being for the most part floated down the river.

The Railway has ten stations and stopping places; thus the distance between each is very short. The service on most of the stations is performed by a station-master only, who has his residence in the station building; he attends to the telegraph, and has access to hired assistance, when necessary for the loading and receiving of the goods, there being with the train an extra guard or two to assist at the stations.   Only at Hamar, the principal terminal station of the Railway, there is, besides the station-master, an office clerk, a telegraph clerk, and seven to eight porters.   There is a local manager of the line, he being also an engineer, resident at Hamar station.

For the traffic there are three tank locomotives, each weighing, with coal and water, 15 tons, with 0.3 tons on the two pair driving wheels.   Of these engines there is rarely more than one used at a time.

The rolling stock consists of 5 passenger carriages, each for 30 seats, 3 brake-vans and 50 goods-waggons, all on 4 wheels each.

For the engine service, there are besides the foreman of the repairing shop, who also has to make duty as a driver when necessary, 1 engine driver, 1 stoker, 2 guards, and 4 workmen in the shop.

For the maintenance of the line, there are 1 permanent way inspector, 4 foremen, and 15 or 16 workmen.

During the third traffic year (1865) there have been conveyed on the line 32,978 passengers, with the receipts of £1385 15s.; the average distance for each passenger being 12 miles.

The amount of goods carried has been 7269 tons only, of which 6-7 has been carried up (in direction from Hamar) and 1-7 down.   The goods have principally consisted of:

Grain,...	2,500 tons
Timber and deals,..............................	2,210 "
Salt, ...	563 "
Iron, ...	446 "
Fish, ...	360 "

The receipts for goods have been.....................£1778 15 0
The receipts for carriages, cattle, parcels, excess of
         luggage, mails and telegrams   183   3 0
Other receipts, about....................................   118   7 0
                                                    _____
            Total receipts,...........................£2080   5 0

or £141 13s. 4d. per English mile, per annum, which undoubtedly is the lowest range of revenue of any passenger Railway.

The expenditure during the same year amounted to £3297,
or £137 7s. 6d. per mile of Railway. Per train mile, the
ballast miles not included, the expenses have been 2s. 7d.

In the above sums are included :

The expenses to the head administration in Christiana, the
    salary to the manager, the wages to the stations service
    and to the conductors £1285 10 0

The expenses to the locomotive department......... 893 10 0

Do   do   carriage department............. 152 0 0

Do   do   permanent way.................. 794 2 0

Do   do   maintenance of the buildings,
                the station grounds, the
                telegraph, &c............... 160 11 0

Sundry expenses 11 7 0

The locomotives have in all run 27,126 English miles, of
which 25,400 with passengers and goods, 1,684 with ballast,
and 42 as assisting engines, including 3 per cent. reckoned for
shunting at stations and sidings.

Generally there is but one train daily up and down. Twice
a week, and at certain times, when the traffic is greater, a
second train, but very rarely a third train, is running.

The expenses of working and maintenance of the engines
have been 7s. 0d. per train mile.

For working the locomotives have been used 281 tons of
coal, or 23.2 lbs. per mile, which has cost £340 5s. 0d. Fire-
wood, candles, oil, waste, &c., to the amount of £89 7s.

All goods waggons are calculated to carry a load of 5 tons
each, but the average load has been 3½ tons only. About 2-5
of the waggons in the train have been moved empty.

The 58 carriages and waggons have in all run 150,520 carriage miles. The expenses of maintenance have therefore
been not fully ¼d. per English mile.

On an average, every train has consisted of 2 passenger
carriages, 1 brake van, and 3 goods waggons.

The engines can take 15 waggons in the train, but the traffic is at present so small that, on an average, three goods waggons only are taken, besides 2 passenger carriages, and I brake and luggage van.

The cause of the inconsiderable traffic and small receipts of this Railway is the poor and thinly populated districts, in connection with the shortness of the line, which makes travellers and goods intended to go to or from distant places to be carried by their own conveyances the whole way, in preference to waiting for the train to be conveyed over a comparatively short distance. The working of the line is necessarily arranged in the cheapest and most economic manner, and by this we have succeeded to cover the expenses by the receipts, while the surplus has been very inconsiderable. In the meantime it is intended soon to extend the Railway, by which the receipts will increase at a comparatively greater rate.

Dr. O. T. BROCK.

List showing the comparative cost of construction, amount of work and equipment of Railways in Norway.

	Kristiania Mjosen. 4 ft. 8½ in. Gauge.		Lillestrom Grandsen. 4 ft. 8½ in. Gauge.		Hamar Grundset. 3 ft. 6 in. Gauge.		Throndhjem Storen. 3 ft. 6 in. Gauge.		Drammen Randsfjord 3 ft. 6 in. Gauge.		Not yet b'ilt Christiania Drammen. 3 feet 6 in. Gauge.	
	Expenses per mile, Norw. Species.	Per cent.	Expenses per mile, Norw. Species.	Per cent.	Expenses per mile, Norw. Species.	Per cent.	Expenses per mile, Norw. Species.	Per cent.	Expenses per mile, Norw. Species.	Per cent.	Expenses per mile, Norw. Species.	Per cent.
The Ground............			7397	3.98	2851	2.8	8822	5.27	7034	4.99	32031	14.7
Fencing			2678	1.44	2801	2.8	2323	1.33	1609	1.14	2643	1.2
Rock and Earthwork....			56839	30.56	30355	29.8	60175	35.94	44989	31.94	75754	34.8
Bridges and Viaducts....			10214	5.49	3241	3.2	19552	11.68	11080	7.86	16480	7.6
Deviation of Roads, etc..			2030	1.09	894	0.9	1615	0.96	1489	1.06	3577	1.7
Permanent Way & Ballast			50759	27.29	29424	28.9	33572	20.05	27862	19.78	27524	12.6
Stations			13345	7.17	12823	12.6	14095	8.42	10357	7.35	12951	6.0
Rolling Stock...........			20950	11.26	13461	13.2	10165	6.07	12625	8.96	16971	7.8
Telegraph..............			1099	0.59	837	0.8	638	0.38	676	0.48	749	0.3
Sundry Expenses.......			527	0.28			1327	0.79	3738	0.03	518	0.2
Engin'ring & Supervision			201714	10.85	5105	5.0	15160	9.05	23109	16.41	28380	13.1
Expenses per mile	370120		186009	100	101792	100	167442	100	140867	100	217578	100
Length in Miles.........	6		10.13		3.4		4.3		8		4.54	
Total Cost.............	2220720		1884275		346095		720000		1126939		987805	

In the above for the Lillestrom-Grandsen line not included the 55000 specie for the Rolling Stock.

No. of Stations..........	11		12		9		10		11		10	
do. per mile........	1.83		1.3		2.6		2.3		1.4		2.2	
No. of Engines..........	12		9		3		4		6		5	
do. per mile........	2		0.9		0.88		0.93		0.75		1.1	
Driving Wheel Pressure in Ton per mile.......	40.8		12.75		9.9		11.2		9.8			
No. of Passenger Car'ages	40		35		8		10		15		26	
do. per mile........	6.66		3.5		2.35		2.3		1.9		5.73	
do. of Seats per mile.	200		93.6		47		56		43			
Each Goods Truck carries	5.94 tons		5.94		5		5		5		5	
No. of Goods Waggons...	322		272		50		60		145		78	
do. per mile........	53.7		26.9		14.8		14		18.12		17.18	
Total carrying capacity of Goods Waggons in tons	1912.7		1615		250		300		7.25		390	
do. per mile........	318.8		159.4		73.5		69.8		90.6		85.9	
No. of Passengers carried one year..............	156145		82189		32978		62987					
Passenger Mile per Mile Road................	78618		36948		16345		34071					
Total Receipts in Norw. Species..............	229462		66619		15301		24542					
Receipts per mile, Norw. Species..............	38244		8766		4500		5708					
Receipts per Train mile, Norw. Species	13.28		5.76		4.23		4.77					
Total Expenses, Norw. Species..............	112382		67818		14837		23438					
Do. per mile, Norw. do..	18730		8923		4364		5450					
Do. per Train mile	7.78		5.86		4.10		4.55					
Dividend................	5.27pr.ct		0.08		0.12		0.15					
Goods moved in Tons....	207906		62621		8748		11614					
Ton mile per mile of Line	106694		35775		6290		10056					

N.B.—1 Norwegian Mil (Mile)—7 English Miles.
1 Species equals 111 American cents, or 4s. 6d. English.

C. PIHL.

(Copy.)

Particulars for the 3 ft. 6 inch Gauge Railways in Norway.

	Hamar-Elverum Railway.	Throndhjem Storen Railway.	Drammen Randsfjord Railway.	Kongsvinger Railway.
Length of line in Eng. miles...	24½	30.1	56	71
Bill passed for its construct'n·	1857	1857	1863	{ Half length. 1857 and 1863.
Opened for traffic......... {	24 / 6.62	} ¾.64 {	15 / 11.66 Half length	1 / 10.62 and 4 / 1.65
Width of Gauge.............	3′ 6″ Eng.	3′ 6″ Eng.	3′ 6″ Eng.	4′ 8½″ Eng.
Sharpest Curve, Radius......	900′ N.	750′ N.	900 N.	1250 N.
Curves often occuring......	1000	900	1000	1500
Width of formation line......	12½ N.	12½ N.	12½ N.	18 N.
Width on top of ballast	8 N.	8 N.	8 N.	12 N.
Thickness of ballast.........	1.8 N.	1.8 N.	1.8 N.	2 N.
Weight of rail.................	36 lbs. per yard.	36 & 41 lbs. per y'd.	40 lbs. per yard.	62 lbs. per yard.
Kind of sleepers.............	O of 8 x 9 (pine.)	O of 8 & 9″ (pine)	O of 9″ (pine)	O of 9 x 10 (pine)
Length of sleepers...........	6′ 6″ N.	6′ 6″ N.	6′ 6″ N.	9′ N.
Distance apart	2′ 9″ and 2′ 6″ N.	"	"	3′ N.
Kind of fastening...........	Dogspikes 5″ En.	"	"	Dogspike, 5½′ E.
Fishing................... {	{ 2 plates 11½ Eng. long, and 4⅝″ bolts.	} "	"	{ 15″ plates and 4½ bolts.
Number of stations	9	10	11	12
Number per mile	0.37	0.33	0.2	0.17
Number of engines	3	4	6	9
Do do per mile..	0.12	0.13	0.11	0.13
Available weight for traction and driving wheels in tons..	33	47	77.7	129
Do do per mile..	1.35	1.56	1.4	1.8
No. of carriages.............	8	10	15	35
Do do per mile	0.3	0.33	0.3	0.5
Seats	6.7	9.02	6.2	13.4
No. of goods-waggons.......	50	60	145	272
Do do per mile..	2.04	2	2.6	3.8
Carrying capacity, per mile, in tons	10.2	10	12.9	23
Expenses—Head office, 1 year.	£310	£479	} Only half the	{ £453
For working the traffic. Stations, one year........	1146	1170	line tempo-	3643
Locomotive Dep't, 1 year.	894	} 1458	rarily open-	5235
Waggon " "	152		ed for traffic	2078
Maintenance of line and bridges, 1 year	794	2100	this year.	3662
Expence total	3296	5207		15071
Receipts—per annum	3400	5785		14804
No. of train miles	25333	41573		81032
Total cost of construction....	76979	160000	£255,528	480950
Of which in per cent for ground	2.8	5.27	4.9	3.8
Fencing	2.7	1.39	1.1	1.4
Substructure	29.8	35.94	31.3	29.6
Bridges & viaducts	3.3	11.68	7.7	5.3
Permanent way.......	28.9	20.05	19.4	26.5
Stations.............	12.6	8.42	9.3	6.9
Road crossings and deviations	0.9	0.96	1.0	1.0
Telegraph............	0.8	0.38	0.4	0.6
Locomotive carriages & waggons	13.2	6.07	8.8	14.1
Engineering and expenses not calculated	5.0	9.84	16.1	10.8
Cost of Construction per mile.	£3142	£5312	£4563	£6070

1 Norw. foot = 1.0297 Eng. F.

NOTE.—The price in " Engineering " (£6350) refers to the 56 miles to Kongsvinger, before the extension of the line to Sweden.

C. PIHL.

Christiana, April 12th, 1867.

To G. LAIDLAW, Esq., Toronto, C. W.

Table showing characteristics of Lines of 3 ft. 6 in. Gauge which have been constructed up to present time.

Name of Railway.	Length of Line, English Miles.	Cost per Mile, £1 sterling=$5.00.	Weight of Rails, per lineal yard.	Nature of Joint.	Size of Sleepers.	Formation Width.	Steepest Gradient.	Radius of Sharpest Curve.	Ordinary Speed, Miles per hour.	Greatest recorded Speed, miles per hour.	Number of Stations.	Weight of Engines.	Cost of Engines.	No. of Passenger Cars.	No. of Freight Cars.	Remarks.
Norwegian Railways. Hamar Line	24½	$15,000	37 lbs.	Fish'd	6 ft. 6" x 10" x 5"	13 ft.	1 in 70	1000 ft.	15	...	8	14 tons	...	6	50	Besides the 8 Stations there are Carriage Sheds and a Repair Shop. Ballast Waggons and Tools for repairs are included in cost. "Although the works were not of a heavy character, there were many difficulties to contend with, the Line having to avoid upwards of 400 ft. and cross extensive and deep swamps.
Throndhjem Line	31¼	$25,000	37 & 41 lbs.	do.	6 ft. 6" x 10" x 5"	13 ft.	1 in 42	750 ft.	15	...	11	14 tons	...	8	60	Ballast Waggons, and Tools for repairs, besides Carriage and Goods Sheds, and a Repair Shop, are included in cost given. The Line runs through a difficult country, and "required many heavy works of construction, among which were numerous large bridges, some being from 70 to 100 ft. high; several cuttings containing from 50,000 to 70,000 cub. yds. each, and others through rock of more than 30 ft. in depth." The 41 lbs. rails were used only on the steep inclines.
Swedish Railways. Uttersborg Line	23	$9,500	37 lbs.	do.	6 ft. 6" x 8" x 5"	13 ft.	1 in 100	1000 ft.	16	30	6	13 tons	$7,000	50	50	There are other Narrow Gauge Lines in Sweden, of which the Uttersborg Line may be taken as the type. Stock of Swedish manufacture.
Queensland Railways. Ipswick, Toowoomba and Dalby Line	130	$60,000	40 lbs.	do.			1 in 40	350 ft.	20	25	15	15 tons	$7,050			On the 78 miles between Ipswick and Toowoomba the works are unusually heavy. "The sides of the range are cut up by very numerous and deep ravines, and their slopes very steep. On this section there are 11 tunnels, one of them over ¼ of a mile in length, and "an amount of bridging and water ways has had to be provided, greater, perhaps, than in any 78 miles of Railway yet made in any country." The country presents ordinary difficulties only. The Engineer of Queensland Railways says, in his report, "The difficulty of procuring labour and materials was very great, and the rate of wages very high." Rolling Stock sent from England.
Toowoomba & Warwick Line	62	$30,000	40 lbs.	do.								15 tons	$7,050			All the "Material" and Stock for this Line was sent from England.
India (Madras). Arconum and Conjeveram	19	$17,500								40?						

J. EDWD. BOYD.

March, 1867.

Mr. Boyd says in his pamphlet: "The cost of a railway is,
"all other conditions being similar, controlled to a great ex-
"tent by the gauge. Assuming a gauge of 5 feet 6 inches
"for Trunk lines, it by no means follows that for tributary
"lines and independent lines, in country districts, a narrow
"gauge (say 3 feet) might not be introduced with advantage.
"It is conceded that the resistance due to curves decreases as
"the width between the rails is reduced, as sharper curves
"could therefore be introduced without a corresponding in-
"crease in the resistance.

"Heavy earthworks could be avoided, without resort to
"steep gradients, and narrow gauge tributaries could be car-
"ried into many districts when lines of the wider gauge
"would be enormously expensive, in both construction and
"operation.

"This reduction of the gauge would be followed by a dim-
"inution of the cost of every part of the road, from the *turning*
"*of the first sod to the driving of the last spike*, as follows:—
"Saving on earth, 50 per cent.; on masonry, 25 per cent.;
"the engines would weigh from twelve to fourteen tons, in-
"stead of twenty-eight tons; and the weight of the rails,
"chairs, &c., being proportionately less, the cost of permanent
"way *would be about one-half*, with a corresponding reduction
"in the cost of rolling stock.

"The railway of narrowest gauge used for passenger traffic,
"worked by locomotives, is in Merionethshire, Wales—gauge,
"2 feet. Between June, 1863, and February, 1865, the four
"engines employed on this road (7½ tons) had run 57,000
"miles without leaving the rails—the steepest gradient being
"1 in 60. Up these gradients, these engines take a load of
"50 tons at ten miles an hour; sharpest curves on the line,
"132 feet radius.

"In the colliery districts of England and Wales there are
"lines of 2 feet 4 inches, 2 feet 6 inches, and 2 feet 8 inches,
"which are used with great success.

"The Norwegian lines have a gauge of 3 feet 6 inches; en-
"gines weigh 14 tons; speed 15 miles an hour. A gauge of
"3 feet 9 inches has been successfully worked in Belgium.
"Upon a line three feet gauge, passenger trains could be run
"at 15 to 20 miles an hour, the carriages being say 7 feet 6
"inches wide inside—ample room for comfortable seats—less
"width would answer freight cars."

" Mr. Fitzgibbon, Chief Engineer to the Government of Queensland, Australia, states :—' A railway of 3 feet 6 inches " ' gauge will accommodate a traffic of 400 tons of goods and " ' 800 passengers in each twelve hours.

" ' During the nine months ending 30th September, 1866, " ' the average daily traffic on the E. & N. A. Railway was " ' 484 passengers and 185 tons freight, and on the N. S. Rail- " ' way, 400 passengers and 180 tons freight.

" ' On 22 miles of one line, when it passes over the Little " ' Liverpool and Main Ranges, numerous curves of 5 chains " ' radius are introduced, in order to avoid the heavy works in " ' excavation, tunnelling, viaducts, &c., which the use of curves " ' of a larger radius would involve ; but had a gauge of 4 feet " ' $8\frac{1}{2}$ inches been adopted, curves of 8 chains radius (as used in " ' crossing the Blue Mountains in New South Wales) would· " ' have been necessary ; and it was found, on a calculation of " ' the quantities of work, that the cost of the line with 4 feet " ' $8\frac{1}{2}$ inch gauge would exceed that of the 3 feet 6 inch gauge " ' by more than three-fold.

" ' Taking the item of permanent way, we find that on the " ' New South Wales lines the cost per mile is £2,996 7s. 6d. ; " ' while on one 3 feet 6 inch gauge line the cost is £2,162 4s. 0d. " ' per mile, including broken stone ballast ; giving a difference " ' of £834 per mile in favour of the narrow gauge. '

" A statement which is appended to the report shows that, " taking an equal quantity of rolling stock on each line, the " cost of that of the 3 feet 6 inch gauge is $64\frac{1}{2}$ per cent. of the " cost on the 4 feet 6 inch gauge.

" It appears that a speed of over 20 miles an hour has been " attained on the 3 feet 6 inch line, without any perceptible " oscillation or unsteadiness of the carriages, which are roomy " and comfortable, and give the greatest satisfaction to the " public.

" *Mr. Fitzgibbon maintains* ' *that it is the wisest possible policy* " ' *to provide only for the wants we now foresee, and to carry out* " ' *effectually a system of railways which is within our present* " ' *means, leaving posterity to decide what further expenditure* " ' *should be incurred to meet its wants.*

" ' Again, to expend two or three times the necessary amount " ' now, with a view to meeting a want which cannot be felt for " ' perhaps twenty years or more, is simply to expend in inter- " ' est alone a sum sufficient to re-build an entirely new system " ' of communication.

"'The construction of the road, and the various appliances "'employed, are in all respects equal to any railway in the "'world, excepting only that they are limited in power to the "'wants of the case.'"

Mr. Boyd contends that if the diminution of cost is so great as between a 3 feet 6 inch gauge and one of 4 feet 8 inches, the difference between one of 3 feet and of 5 feet 6 inches is certainly not over-estimated at 50 per cent.

The same author remarks, in a subsequent letter, that "after fully discussing the matter, the Swedish engineers "have decided upon a 3 feet 6 inch gauge for all local lines or "feeders—and several of such having been built during the "last few years, are giving entire satisfaction.   In one of those "the embankments are 13 feet broad; weight of rails, 37 lbs. "per yard, connected with fish plates; speed 16 miles an hour, "but occasionally brought up to 30 and 35 miles an hour."

"THE 3 FEET 6 INCH RAILWAY GAUGE.
"To the Editor of 'Engineering.'

" Sir,—By request of my friend, Mr. C. Pihl, Chief Engineer "of the Norwegian Government Railways, I beg to hand you "the enclosed paper on the 3 ft. 6 in. railway gauge, and "knowing well the trustworthiness of his practical experience, "I have no doubt that by inserting it in your valuable peri-"odical much additional light would be thrown on the question "to which it relates.

"I remain, Sir, your obedient Servant,
"W. Tottie."

"Royal Swedish and Norwegian Consulate-General,
    "London, March 7, 1867.

": Sir,—In 'Engineering,' of 4th January, I find, in an ar-"ticle headed 'Railways in Lilliput,' views with regard to the 3 "feet 6 inch gauge railway system (as carried out in Queens-"land, India, and Norway), which are so much at variance "with the experience gained in this country, where railways ".of this description have been in full operation since 1861, "that you will allow me, no doubt, as the engineer of the lines, "to make a few remarks, which may possibly be acceptable to "those of your readers who feel interested in this matter.

"In your article you ask what was to compensate for the "manifest disadvantages of the 3 feet 6 inch gauge, and for an "answer refer to a letter which Mr. William T. Downe, Memb.

" Inst. C.E., has lately published in Queensland, in which he
" says he considers that the safe maximum speed on the 3 ft.
" 6 in. gauge cannot exceed ten, or, at most, twelve miles an
" hour, and that, although he has travelled twenty-two miles
" an hour on this gauge, he doubts whether the working stock
" would admit of it, except in the case of the engine running
" down steep gradients; and he states that he would feel more
" at his ease on a line of ordinary gauge at 50 miles an hour.
" He further says:—'In Queensland the features of the country
" enforce the use of five-chain curves, and consequently a 3 ft.
" 6 in. gauge.'   On this you make the following remarks:
" ' Before engineers inflict a wholly insufficient gauge upon the
" railway system of a colony, they should first ascertain
" whether, even with curves of minimum radii, rolling stock
" cannot be constructed to work them upon the ordinary
" gauge;' and, in concluding your article, yo say that the same
" remarks apply to India and Norway.

" With regard to the information received from, and opin-
" ions formed on the Queensland Railway, it is not for me to
" make any remark, except when they effect the system, and
" are at variance with facts gained by experience.   My inten-
" tions are not, however, to enter into any polemical discussion,
" as the 4 ft. 8½ in. as well as the 3 ft. 6 in. gauge systems
" have been in operation here for many years.   There is no
" doubt or uncertainty with us about the question at issue;
" and I will, therefore, merely give facts and results as supple-
" mentary to the information you are already in possession of
" from Queensland, and which may be of interest to those who
" wish to investigate the subject.

" When it is said that the adoption of the narrow gauge has
" been enforced by the necessity for sharp curves, the conjec-
" ture is not quite in accordance with the facts of the case
" here, as we have hitherto been able to avoid curves of less
" than 11 chains.   *With us it has been a question of providing*
" *a railway communication at a comparatively small cost in a*
" *country of large extent, with little traffic and limited resources;*
" *and although the greater facility of traversing sharp curves is*
" *a decided and no unimportant advantage to be gained by the use*
" *of the small gauge, this consideration has not enforced its adop-*
" *tion here.   It has been in this case the choice between a cheap*
" *and efficient railway or none.*

" With what success these lines have been carried out we

3

" shall see. I will now give the cost of three separate rail-
" ways, which I built at the same time, under equal circum-
" stances, and with the same view as to economy and efficency;
" the one line, the Kongsvinger line, of 4 ft. 8½ in. gauge, with
" a length of fifty-six miles, has cost £6,350 per mile, includ-
" ing stations and rolling stock, but no workshops; the Hamar-
" Elverum line, of 3 ft. 6 in. gauge, and twenty-four miles only,
" has cost £3,142 per mile, including stations, rolling stock,
" and small workshops; the third line, the Throndjem-Storen
" Railway, also of 3 ft. 6 in. gauge, and thirty-one and a half
" miles long, has cost £5,300, including everything. At the
" present time there are fifty-six miles more (the Dramman-
" Randsfjord Railway, of the same narrow gauge) under con-
" struction, the half of which is temporarily opened for traffic.
" This line is calculated at £4,563 per mile, and for this sum
" I have no doubt it will be completed. On the two last-
" named lines the works are comparatively very heavy; the
" country which we have had to go through has been difficult
" to deal with, and necessitated many extensive works, such
" as cuttings (to a great extent in hard rock), frequent bridges
" and viaducts, some of timber and some of iron, several ex-
" ceeding 70 feet in height and of considerable length. Be-
" sides these, there are extensive and comparatively costly
" stone works along the declivities by the side of the rivers
" and hills.

" The regular trains are run here at 14 miles an hour, in-
" cluding stoppages, or 16 to 20 miles between stations, the
" very same speed at which the mixed trains run on the 4 ft.
" 8½ in. gauge here. As to the safety of fast running, engines
" and carriages appear to run as safely and steadily at 30 miles
" an hour on the 3 ft. 6 in. gauge as they do on one of 4 ft. 8½
" in., and I have run the very engine illustrated in your jour-
" nal of 21st December last at upwards of 40 miles an hour,
" with as much feeling of ease and security as I have felt
" when running any engine on a broader gauge. The engines,
" as well as the rest of the rolling stock, are constructed with
" an angle of stability fully as great as in rolling stock for an
" ordinary gauge; this, with a sufficient minimum load on the
" axle, being the principal condition for stability, leaves the
" gauge as a factor of practically small importance in limiting
" the speed. The working stock, when substantially and ju-
" diciously constructed, is as durable in one case as in the other.

" In stating these facts it is not my intention to advocate as
" high a speed on these lines, with light engines of only 3 ft.
" to 3 ft. 9 in. driving wheels, as on lines of a broader gauge;
" they are not designed for high speed, but to suit circum-
" stances where this is of a secondary consideration.

" When the difficulties in the construction of an efficient
" rolling stock for this gauge have been satisfactorily over-
" come, the one gauge being as empirical as the other, it then
" becomes in my opinion the duty of the engineer to decide
" which gauge is best adapted to the requirements of the
" country. If the 4 ft. 8½ in. gauge is sufficient for a country
" with vast traffic and ample resources, the 3 ft 6 in. gauge
" may be all that is required in places less favourably situated.
" Should, however, that fortunate time arrive (say in the course
" of fifteen or twenty years), when the traffic has developed
" itself to such an extent that the line, as originally construct-
" ed, proves insufficient, then I believe that a double line
" would naturally suggest itself as meeting the requirements
" of increased traffic in every way better than a single line of
" wider gauge. The cost of the addition would, based upon
" calculations made for this purpose, be rather more than 50
" per cent. (without much variation) of the original cost of the
" line proper, stations and rolling stock not included, and the
" total of this double line would then cost about the same as
" the single 4 ft, 8½ in. would originally have cost. I can,
" therefore, not see the necessity or justice of having the gauge
" wider to suit increasing demands in the one case rather than
" in the other, as long as there is the same facility of adding
" proportionally to the working power. There is certainly a
" greater difference in the producing capabilities or the traffic
" of the various countries than there is here in the gauges.
" What may befit one country, is therefore not in place in an-
" other, and it therefore is necessary here, as elsewhere, to
" adapt the means to the end. The amount of interest on the
" difference in the original outlay between the two lines would
" consequently have been lost during the assumed period,
" besides the excess of expense of keeping up the wider line.

" In proof of the slight difference in the cost of the two sys-
" tems, there has been adduced the amount of earthwork in a
" bank 50 ft. high, the formation width of which has been
" set down at 14 ft. in one case and 12 ft. in the other. This I
" cannot consider fair. The formation width for the line of 4

"ft. 8½ in. gauge is generally from 15 ft. to 18 ft., say 16½ ft.
"on an average (it is here 18 ft.), and for the 3 ft. 6 in. gauge
"it is here 12 ft. 6 in. (The reason why the latter is reduced
"so much, I suppose, is obvious). The average height of the
"banks and cuttings on the narrower gauge is less than on the
"broad, owing to the greater facility of adaptation to the
"country. With us the height is ten ft., whereas, had the
"broader gauge been adopted, it would have been 12 ft. to 14
"ft., say 13 ft. This would make, with the same slope as in
"your example, the proportion as 225 to 383 1 7, or nearly as
"4 to 7, instead of 31 to 32, as stated. You have, however,
"used the slope 1 to 1, which would make my figures less
"favourable than the above.

"I find that I have already gone more at length into this
"discussion than was my intention, and am prepared for
"doubts being entertained as to the correctness of the con-
"clusions which I arrived at from the facts here set forth.

"Of many to whom the subject may be of real importance,
"few will probably be able personally to study the subject on
"the spot in India and Queensland; but with the present easy
"communication between England and this country, any
"one willing to devote nine or ten days to the purpose may
"conveniently see and judge for himself; and I can assure all
"such visitors that they will meet with every facility for ob-
"taining all the information they may desire.

"I am, Sir,
"Yours respectfully,
"C. PIHL.

"Christiana, February 25, 1867."

The following extracts from a letter received from the eminent
English engineering firm, Sir Charles Fox & Son, bearing directly
on the question in hand, will be read with much interest, and
will command the attention due to the statements and opinions of gentlemen of such world-wide experience and high
standing:—

"We have been requested by Mr. Middleton to communi-
"cate with you upon the subject of Light Railways, which we
"have much pleasure in doing, as this is a matter to which we
"have given much attention.

"We are the Consulting Engineers to the Colonial Govern-
"ment of Queensland, which is now engaged in constructing

"upwards of 200 miles of railway of 3 ft. 6 in.—of which 50
"miles have been for some time open for traffic—and has also
"under survey some 200 miles more. These lines are for the
"most part made through an undeveloped country, for
"the purpose of opening it up, and for a portion of their
"length pass through very mountainous districts, involving
"heavy works.

"The principle adopted on these lines is to make them in
"the very best manner, to spare no necessary expense to en-
"sure materials and workmanship of first-class quality, but so
"to adapt them in every way to the traffic to be expected,
"without the evil generally accompanying such economy, of
"heavy working and maintenance expenses. These lines are
"suitable for Passenger and Goods traffic with trains weighing
"150 tons gross, exclusive of the locomotives, travelling at an
"average speed, including stoppages, of 20 miles per hour.
"They are laid with iron rails weighing 40 lbs. to the yard,
"flat-bottomed, properly fished at the joints, and secured with
"fang-bolts and dog-spikes to traverse rectangular hard-wood
"sleepers 2' 6" to 3' 0" apart from centre to centre. The
"bridges, which are very numerous and heavy for the most
"part, have lattice girders of wrought iron. The chief stations
"are also of wrought iron lined with wood, and have been sent
"out complete from this country. The rolling stock is of the
"very best description, and the passenger carriages quite equal
"for comfort to the best in this country. The locomotives
"weigh from 15 to 16 tons when ready for the road, and are
"capable of travelling with ease at the working speed and with
"the load before referred to, on ruling gradients of 1 in 100,
"with curves of 330 ft. radius. By the use, however, of loco-
"motives of a slightly heavier class, gradients of 1 in 40 can be
"worked with ease with similar curves.

"The ruling principle throughout is, that no wheel shall,
"under any circumstances, have more than three tons upon
"it, and that the speed shall not exceed a maximum of 30
"miles per hour, and every detail is adapted to these data.

"We have also, in conjunction with another Engineer, con-
"structed a line in India upon the 3'6" gauge, as a tributary
"to the Madras Railway. This line passes through an easy
"country, excepting that there were a good many bridges, in
"order to provide water-way. The land was provided by the
"Government, and the works were carried out by the Com-

"pany's own Engineer.   The rails weigh 36 lbs. to the yard,
" laid on traverse teak sleepers.   The rolling stock and engines
" are only so far different from those used in Queensland as is
" necessary to meet the difference of climate.   The stations
" are large bungalows, with ample accommodation.   The line
" is single, with passing places.   *The total cost of the works, in-*
" *cluding freight from England, management, &c., has been only*
" *£3,200 per mile, or, including rolling stock, stations and stores,*
" *£3,800 per mile.   The line has now been worked for some time*
" *most satisfactorily, the trains having on several occasions at-*
" *attained a speed of 40 miles an hour, and the working expenses*
" *being moderate.*"

The following testimony from Major Adelskold, himself an
unwilling convert to the Light Narrow Gauge system, is most
important, in so far as it relates to the questions of snow and
transhipment, points upon which the opponents of the Narrow
Gauge Toronto, Grey and Bruce, and Toronto and Nipissing
Railways base a good deal of needless opposition :

" The line from Uttensburg to Koping is twenty-three miles
" long.   The gauge is 3 feet 6 inches, the embankments are
" 13 feet broad ; the weight of rails 37 lbs. per yard, connected
" with fish plates.   The inclines are favorable.   The sharpest
" curve is of 1,000 feet radius.   Including the termini there
" are six stations with all necessary buildings, containing
" waiting rooms, booking offices, warehouses, apartments for
" station masters, as well as side rails, turn-tables, crossings,
" &c.   The rolling stock, entirely of Swedish manufacture,
" consists of three locomotives and fifty carriages and wag-
" gons for passengers and goods.   The general speed of each
" train is sixteen miles per hour, but it has on several occa-
" sions been brought up to thirty and thirty-five miles per
" hour, when both carriages and waggons moved with perfect
" steadiness.

" Besides this Railway, there are at present several Narrow
" Gauge Lines in existence in Sweden, trafficked by locomo-
" tives, extending in length to 158 miles, all of which have
" proved fully equal to the traffic and the expectations of their
" promoters.   Two of these Narrow Gauge lines are branches
" of the main Government lines, one from Herljunga to Boras,
" twenty-six miles, and the other to Wenersborg and Udde-

" walla, fifty-six miles long. Before the first of these lines
" was opened for traffic, it was generally imagined that the
" reloading of goods from one Railway to another would in-
" volve considerable expenses and waste of time. *This in-*
" *convenience has, however, since proved of but trifling impor-*
" *tance, as the cost of reloading goods from one waggon to another,*
" *under a special shed, when the waggons are placed alongside*
" *of one another, does not exceed one penny per ton.*

" Another dislike which I myself entertained against the
" Narrow Gauge was that the smaller and lighter locomo-
" tives should not be able to keep the line open in winter; but
" experience during several severe winters has shown that,
" with suitably constructed snow ploughs, the Narrow Gauge
" lines *have been kept as free from snow as the broader ones.*
" *The Narrow Gauge may thus be said to have given satisfactory*
" *results in Sweden.* Its principal advantage is in original
" cost, which is so considerably below that of a broader gauge.
" The working expenses have also been considerably lower,
" partly because the resistance in the curves with the same
" speed diminishes in proportion with the gauge, partly, also,
" because the dead weight of the carriages comparatively
" diminishes with the gauge; and finally because the lighter
" locomotives on a Narrow Gauge line do not wear out the
" rails so easily as a heavier engine on a broader gauge."

The evidence in favour of the Light Railways from Norway
and Sweden is of the highest character and importance. The
climate of Canada, Sweden and Norway, is the same, and the
timber business, in both countries, constitutes a large portion
of the traffic of the local roads. On these points the testimony
of the Norwegian and Swedish engineers leaves not a doubt
of the suitableness and effectiveness of these Light Narrow
Gauge Railways to the climate, traffic, and means of building
Railways of this country.

The distance of the counties of Bruce, Grey, North Ontario
and Victoria from leading markets, renders unprofitable the
cultivation of a surplus over local wants of barley, peas, oats,
and roots, and the average price of these articles rules so low,
that they will not generally pay reasonable cost for produc-
tion, and heavy charges for carriage over bad roads, to distant

markets. Wheat, pork, butter and ashes, being greater value in less bulk, bear high charges for teaming better than the coarser kinds of farm produce. Without water or Railroad communications, the products of the forest, raw or manufactured, are nearly *valueless*. The greater portion of the wheat, in the counties of Grey and Bruce, is bought in winter, for less than its relative value, because it cannot be moved until spring, and has to be held a long time, subject to heavy charges for interest, insurance, and storage, a loss further augmented by the caution of bankers and dealers, who require and will have plenty of margin to cover such long risks. These circumstances, together with the fear of hot weather affecting the condition of the wheat, diminish competition to the detriment of the producer.

What most retards the settlement of our wild lands, is the time and labour required to burn the timber, which is done at a cost of $14 per acre, while, if railroad facilities were afforded the settlers, they could sell it at remunerative prices.

In the city of Toronto, there is consumed annually about 350,000 dollars' worth of cordwood, and coals imported to the value of $200,000; half these large amounts would find its way into the hands of the farmers, if the present and projected Railways were bound by law to afford the same facilities to the cordwood trade which is extended to the lumber business.

The value would be very great to the proprietors of land, on the routes of the new Railways, of a market at each station, for fuel for the Railways, and for the city of Toronto, when $2 or $3 cash could be had for every cord, and market prices for stave and square timber, as well as lumber.

The loss is incalculable to the districts traversed by the G. W. R., G. T. R., and N. R., because these roads have not afforded facilities for the conversion of cordwood into money, and consequently, now unbroken wilds into cultivated fields. The increase of traffic would have more than repaid any advance in the cost of the fuel for their engines. The people, by legislation, ought to compel these railway companies to carry cordwood on an equitable basis.

About 40,000 cords of wood were exported to Charlotte for fuel for the N. Y. Central Railway last season, that influential Corporation having secured a reduction of the duty. Proper facilities being afforded for carrying on this trade, it would largely increase. The competition engendered by it, and the exhaustion of supplies near navigable water, are the causes of the present high prices of cordwood.

The 'yearly chopping' of the black counties, sold at $2 per cord, would bring more money, *low transport being available, than all their crops of cereals, excepting wheat,* much as we may be surprised at the statement. Bush land in the front townships, near navigable water, is now more valuable than old cleared land; and this would be the case with land near railroads, if they would carry wood at fair rates.

In settlements, a market for timber of all kinds—lumber, staves, shingles, hoops, bark, and fencing stuffs—is of paramount importance, as by this means the struggling farmers are enabled to *cash their labour*, and with the money obtained provide themselves with household necessities, seed, cattle, &c., which are obtained with great difficulty when the first crops on the new clearings fail, from any cause, to meet the requirements of the case.

In the State of Maine, some railways have little or no other kind of traffic than the carriage of lumber, wood and bark.

The following report on the Cordwood business on the European and North American Railway, N. B., will be interesting, as it proves to the citizens of Toronto that they could have wood at $4 delivered in Toronto:—

"LIGHT RAILWAYS AND THE CORDWOOD QUES-"TION.

"European and N. American R. R.

"General Supt.'s Office,
"St. John, N. B., August 15, 1867.

"James G. Worts, Esq., President Board of Trade, To-"ronto:

"Sir,—At the time I was in Toronto, not being 'prepared

" with any notes, I could not give you much definite informa-
" tion on the 'Cordwood Question,' which seems to occupy
" such a prominent place in the discussions on your Light
" Railway scheme.   I beg leave now to furnish you with some
" notes on the subject, deduced from the traffic on this line
" during the past six years.

   " The average quantity of Cordwood brought to market has
" been 6,660 cords (128 cubic feet) per annum.   The greatest
" quantity in any one year was 8,180 cords, and the least 5,550
" cords.   The average distance this wood was carried was 33
" miles, and the average freight per cord one dollar.   The value of
" the wood in the St. John market may be taken at about $3 50
" per cord, freight paid.   None of this wood could have been
" brought to market without the railway.   The average yearly
" consumption by the railway is 3,000 cords, for which we have
" paid on an average about $2 40 per cord, delivered at the
" stations.

   " The amount which has been expended annually in the
" district bordering on the railway has therefore been—6,660
" cords sold in St. John market at $2 50 ....$16,650 00
" 3,000 cords sold to railway at $2 40 .... 7,200 00

                                                        _____
                                                        $23,850 00
" The land cleared by the cutting of this quantity of wood
" may be estimated in round numbers at 300 acres per annum.
" This collateral benefit is of more consequence in your cal-
" culations than in ours, as with you every acre cleared is fit
" for agricultural purposes, while with us a great deal of the
" wood grows on hill sides, which are too steep for cultivation.

   " The chief objection to carrying wood by rail is that the
" Company thereby gets up a competition against itself.

   " The St. John market does not, we have found, come into
" competition with us at any point more distant than 45 miles.
" The price we have paid for wood purchased within this limit
" has not exceeded by more than 25 cents per cord the price
" paid at stations beyond.

" The railway has received for freight of
   " wood . ...$6,660 00 per annum
" And assuming that the competition has
      " increased the price on half the quan-
      " tity consumed 25 cents per cord, the
      " loss to the railway has been .... 375 00   do.
                                                _____
                                                $6,285 00 -

"The effect of the competition may be felt more as the
"wood becomes scarcer, but the margin between the profit and
"the loss is so large that it must be some time before they bal-
"ance each other.

"If these notes can be of any use in your estimates of your
"future traffic, I have no objection to your using them in any
"way.

"I am, Sir, yours truly,
"J. EDW. BOYD."

SUBJOINED IS AN ARTICLE FROM THE "TRADE REVIEW" ON
THE CORDWOOD QUESTION.

"The Cordwood question is of vital importance to all the
"inhabitants of all the cities in Upper Canada. Fuel in this
"country takes its position beside wheat as one of the neces-
"saries of life, and anything bearing on its price occurring
"in the various transactions of individuals and companies can-
"not fail to attract general attention. The paper warfare that has
"been raging of late regarding the proposed rival railways
"through the counties between the metropolis of Upper Ca-
"nada and Lake Huron, has brought the Cordwood question
"prominently forward, and Torontonians have been suddenly
"let into one of the secrets by which, for years past, they
"have been heartlessly fleeced and imposed upon and made
"to pay from fifty to seventy-five per cent. more for their
"firing than what they ought—the enormous profits aforesaid
"going to unduly enrich one or two unscrupulous heartless
"speculators. Some such state of things, as is shown by the
"revelations made by Mr. Cumberland, the Managing Direc-
"tor of the Northern Railway Company, and those made by
"Mr. Laidlaw, his opponent, would account, no doubt, for the
"exhorbitant price of Cordwood in every other city in Canada
"as well as Toronto.

"Let it be remembered that Cordwood, during the past
"winter, was selling in Toronto at from $7 50 to $8 per cord.

"The misery that these prohibitory rates entailed on the
"poor, may be better imagined than described. It was so
"great as to produce a public agitation. Then all at once
"railways became philanthropic, corporations became charit-
"able, and a few hundred cords of wood were laid down in
"Toronto for the exclusive use of the poor at from $4 to $5
"per cord. To get it at this rate, however, a series of applica-

" tions and certificates were necessary; in fact, it had to be
" sued for *in forma pauperis*, so that the bulk of the middling
" classes had to buy at $7 or $8 or freeze to death. Mr.
" Cumberland, in his June pamphlet, now tells us with re-
" freshing coolness that all this was unnecessary, and that all
" Toronto, comprising the high, low and middling classes,
" could, and ought to have been supplied with wood last win-
" ter at a rate less than $5 per cord! Hear him:—

" 'It is a fact that we have brought very large supplies of
" Cordwood every year from Innisfil (sixty miles), and deliver-
" ed it in Toronto to the merchants at a prime cost to them of
" $3 84 per cord; and if we add twenty per cent. thereon for
" profit, the selling price would be only $4 60. Again, on one
" occasion we brought down from 700 to 800 cords all the way
" from Collingwood (ninety-four miles), the prime cost of
" which, delivered to the merchants of Toronto, was $4 a cord;
" if we add twenty per cent. for profit, the selling price should
" be $4 80 for a splendid sample of hardwood, brought nearly
" 100 miles.'

" Again, in another place he says:—'We bring in (to Toron-
" to) every year something approaching to 8,000 cords, at costs
" which are quite consistent with a selling price of from $4 50
" to $5.' And as touching the supply of wood that it is abun-
" dant, he argues:—'A short supply simply proves that the
" wood merchants under-estimated the demand, or had no
" capital with which to lay in sufficient stock during the sea-
" son of navigation.'

" Here is an extraordinary state of things. The selling
" price of Cordwood in Toronto ought to have been from $4
" 50 to $5 per cord last winter. It was in reality from $7 50
" to $8! At the first blush one would be inclined to say the
" citizens themselves were to blame; that they lacked energy
" and enterprise; and that they allowed themselves to be
" swindled by a few monopolists. But it is not so. Mr. Laid-
" law's pamphlet explains it. Mr. Cumberland, he says, has told
" only half the truth. Cordwood could be laid down in To-
" ronto at from $4 50 to $5 selling rate, and so it is. Only,
" however, for the benefit of the 'Northern Railway wood
" yard,' and one or two other wood monopolists, who have
" combined to sell to the citizens at from $7 50 to $8 or $9,
" if they can raise the price up to that figure. There is no
" free trade in wood. The Northern Railway will only carry

" the article for their own wood yard, and for the wood yard
" of one or two parties in league with them.   This is substan-
" tiated by the following notice, signed by Mr. Cumberland,
" and distributed at all the stations along the Northern
" line:—

    " 'Notice is hereby given, that in future no Cordwood will
" be received, or allowed to be stacked at the stations, or on
" the side of the track, except only such as is sold and delivered
" under contract to the Company; nor will any Cordwood be
" hereafter carried except from regular stations, nor then ex-
" cept when loaded from the teams direct on the cars.   All
" train rates and special contracts are hereby cancelled.'

    " Besides this prohibitory order, Mr. Laidlaw quotes a cir-
" cular letter addressed by an agent of the Northern Company
" to a few wood monopolists, offering to sell them some thous-
" and cords of wood 'which the Company have to dispose of'
" at various stations along the line.   This letter and the above
" notice fully account for the fact that wood could be laid
" down in Toronto at a selling price of from $4 50 to $5 per
" cord, while in reality the selling price is forced up from $7
" 50 to $8.   There is no competition allowed in wood—no
" free trade in fuel.   As Mr. Laidlaw justly complains:—'A
" citizen cannot buy his year's fuel from a farmer delivered at
" a station on the Northern Railroad, and get it down like a
" car of lumber, timber or wheat.'

    " Now, as we said in the beginning, this question of cheap
" fuel is one that affects every city in Canada.   The Cumber-
" land-Laidlaw revelations prove that in Toronto, at all events,
" fuel could be sold nearly at one-half its present cost if wood
" was dealt with by railways in the same manner as wheat
" or lumber.   For our part, we see no good reason why any
" railway should be allowed to become buyers and sellers as
" well as carriers, or to discriminate against the carriage of an
" article of prime necessity.   If any Railway Company were
" to go into the wheat business, and were to combine with a
" few other monopolists to force up the price of wheat, what a
" shout of indignation would be heard from Sandwich Gaspe!
" If any Railway Company were to issue a notice to all the
" station masters along their line, stating that 'no flour will be
" received or stored at the stations or on the side of the track,
" excepting only such as is sold and delivered under contract
" to the Company,' what a tempest of honest rage would agi-

"tate the land! Yet that is precisely the manner in which
"a leading Railway Company presumes to deal with Cord-
"wood. Is not Cordwood as important an item in the domes-
"tic economy of country and city as wheat and flour? But
"say that it is of less importance, still we can see no justifica-
"tion of the conduct of the Railway Company that refuses to
"carry it. Railway Companies are so far trustees for the
"public, that it would be highly inequitable for them to be-
"come vendors to the public of articles which it is their busi-
"ness to carry for hire, not sell for profit. Besides, in their
"capacity as common carriers they are guilty of a grave breach
"of duty in refusing to carry Cordwood for the public. There
"is a lesson to be learned from the Cumberland-Laidlaw reve-
"lations, and it is this:—Railway Companies ought to be
"compelled to deal with Cordwood as with lumber and wheat.
"This is a period full of railway projects; let the guardians of
"the public interest see that a stringent Cordwood clause is
"inserted in every new charter."

The produce of the part of the western peninsula traversed
by the Grand Trunk, is now, particularly during winter, sub-
jected to inequitably high rates of freight to Toronto.

The Grand Trunk Railroad Company discriminate about 40
per cent. in favour of Montreal and points beyond it, as against
Toronto, although it is the nearest and best market.

The Railway from Durham to Angus would undoubtedly
benefit the district traversed, but it would not benefit Grey
to the extent of half the advantage to be derived from a
Railway on the Central Route, which would be untramelled
by any other policy than the *best* for the local interests *it will
be built to serve.*

There is no reason why Bruce, Western and Northern
Grey, should come under a mortgage to pay 40 per cent. excess of freight on the products of their industry, in the shape
of an everlasting freight tax, to either the proposed Durham
branch of the N. R. R. or the branch of the G. W. R. The
money voted to assist the construction of these roads would
only be a fractional part of the yearly lien of these roads on
the industry of the districts tributary to them, and not half
the benefits would accrue from these branches as from an
independent line, worked in the interests of those counties
and the trade of this city, both interests being fully identical
on this question.

The people of Canada will sooner or later have to take such action as will protect them from being mere 'counters' in the calculation of our Railroad managers. Many of the United States are groaning under railroad tyranny, and some of them, as will be seen from the subjoined extract, are endeavouring to emancipate themselves. The Titusville *Herald* says:

"A committe of the Ohio State Senate has been engaged in overhauling the management of railroads, express companies and telegraph companies. The results of its labours are embodied in a report, containing various recommendations, and in two bills containing such provisions as are necessary to carry out the conclusions to which they have come. They recommend that no railroad company shall be permitted to charge more for a shorter distance than for a longer one; that every company shall publish its tariff of rates and shall adhere to them, and be prohibited under penalties from allowing reductions from it to individual shippers or classes of shippers, and that preference in transportation shall be prohibited, except such as are allowed to live stock, perishable freight, and the like. The committee condemn the policy of freight and express companies having portions of their stock in the hands of railroad officers, and declare that agents and officers of every grade deal with the roads, accept offices and employments inconsistent with their duties, and engage in business which interferes with the rights of the general public. The employment of station agents by express companies is censured, as tending to interfere wifh the rights of the public in the carrying of baggage and parcels on passenger trains, with the interest of the road in its freight traffic, and with the rights of competing express companies. Finally, it is recommended that there shall be appointed a Commissioner of Railways, who shall be charged with the duty of collecting the statistics and the experience of railroad management in the State; of observing its immediate wants and defects; of attending to the enforcement of the law against railroad corporations, and of examining into abuses in railroad affairs, with the view of protecting the rights of the stockholders and of the public."

Toronto is indebted for its pre-eminence as the commercial capital of Upper Canada to its excellent harbour, and the extent and fertility of the country northwards. It is the best market, because the best distributing point for all that part of the peninsula north-west, north and north-east of it. Freights from Toronto to Oswego, Kingston, Cape Vincent, Ogdensburg, and out to seaward, are cheaper, on account of its excellent harbor and other facilities of the port, *than from any other point on the north shore of Lake Ontario.*

These advantages redound to the benefit of all the people who here seek a shipping port or a market. If the rates of freight from all points east of Sarnia and Goderich, to Toronto, were fixed at the same rates as charged from these points to Montreal, Quebec, or Portland, then this city, by virtue of its position and facilities, would receive, and re-ship to other markets, by water or rail, as might suit the interests of the holders (identical with those of the producer) all the products of the districts tributary to the G. T. R. west, better markets often being attainable, at less cost for freight, than those on the line of that road.

The cheapest road to the best markets is what farmers want to find, and having found, it is their interest to support the *establishment of that route, with all their financial, munici-pal, and political strength.*

The Great Western and Grand Trunk Railway Companies have agreed to avoid competition from Guelph, or any other competitive point to Toronto. Therefore, the total rate of freight from Walkerton to Toronto or Hamilton, *via* the Wellington, Grey and Bruce Railway, would necessarily include the *local rate* charged by these roads from Guelph to Hamilton or Toronto, or within a trifle of the *total* rate of freight from Walkerton to Toronto by the Central, or Toronto, Grey and Bruce Railway, a point of the most serious importance to the inhabitants of the counties of Bruce and Grey.

This practical amalgamation, whereby both companies agree to charge their highest local rates, and divide the traffic from Guelph, augurs no good to the people of Wellington, Grey and Bruce, as it deprives them of the advantages to which they are justly entitled, from reasonable competition for their freighting business.

The extra charge of 50 per cent., added to the tariff from Guelph to Toronto, exceeds the amount of all the municipal and general government taxes of the parties affected by this arrangement. The comparison between through rates and local rates, shows the erratic and unfair policy pursued by the Railways towards those who are, and whose children ever will be taxed, to pay the debts incurred for their construction. The produce of Michigan, Illinois, Wisconsin, &c., are carried into and through this country for about half the rates charged for carrying the products of our own farms, subjecting our farmers to disheartening competition, while their produce is also burdened with heavy duties by the people who are so much benefited by cheap through freights on our Trunk lines.

The following letter from Mr. T. C. Chisholm, an extensive produce dealer, and an excellent authority in all matters pertaining to the carrying trade of the country, clearly shows the advantages of the Central Route over either of the other two proposed Routes:—

"SIR,—With this I hand you table of distances and rates of freight.

"TABLE OF DISTANCES,

"Taking Walkerton as the starting point, it will be seen by this table that Walkerton is 12½ miles nearer Toronto *via* the Central (or Toronto, Grey and Bruce) than Hamilton *via* the Wellington, Grey and Bruce, and Great Western; 14 miles nearer Toronto than *via* the Wellington, Grey and Bruce, and Grand Trunk; 44 miles nearer than *via* the Durham and Angus and Northern Railway.

Walkerton to Guelph.. 60 miles.
do.   Hamilton *via* Guelph...............................106½ do.
do.   do.   Toronto and Central (G.W.R.)....133 do.
do.   Toronto do. Guelph and G. T. R.................108 do.
do.   do.   Guelph and G. W. R..............145½ do.
do.   do.   Durham and Angus.................138 do.
do.   do.   Central only........................ 94 do.

4

"TABLE OF RATES.

"Since the traffic arrangement between the Great Western and Grand Trunk Railroads, which came into effect last September, the rates were advanced 50 per cent., and as per their published tariff the freight on grain is 6c. per 60 lbs. to either Hamilton or Toronto; which is 4½c. per ton per mile. Allowing the Wellington, Grey and Bruce the same rate per ton per mile, the freight on grain would be 13¾c. per 60 lbs. to either Hamilton or Toronto. The proposed rate *via* the Toronto, Grey and Bruce is 3c. per ton per mile, or 33⅓ per cent. more than is now charged by the N. R. R. on grain from Lake Huron or Georgian Bay ports, and just double the rate per ton per mile over the winter rate charged by the Grand Trunk to Montreal or Portland, and three times more than their summer rates to the same places. This would make the freight from Walkerton to Toronto on grain 8c. per 60 lbs., or 5½c. per 60 lbs. less than if shipped *via* the Wellington, Grey and Bruce. The same proportion would be saved on all the productions of the country tributary to the Central Road. Allowing the Central to cost $15,000 per mile (an outside price), the road from Toronto to Walkerton would cost $1,410,000—the interest on which would be, at 6 per cent., $84,600—and would only require the County of of Bruce to produce 1,534,000 bushels of grain to pay the interest on the cost of the whole line, Toronto to Walkerton.

"Yours, &c.,

"T. C. CHISHOLM."

The rates of freight on the proposed Grey and Simcoe Railroad should undoubtedly be the same, if not more than those on the Northern Railway, as the latter only pays interest on less than half its cost. It therefore follows that an injustice would be done either company if the rates were reduced below what is now necessary to sustain the Northern Railroad. The subjoined tables are calculated at the *rates per mile charged by the N. R. R. from the proposed junction* at Angus to Toronto:—

Freight from Walkerton to Angus, as per rates charged by N.R.R.	From Angus to Toronto, as per tariff.	Total freight Walkerton to Toronto, *via* Angus.
Lumber, per car...$16.50	......$16 50......	......$33 00......
Staves "...... 16.50	...... 16 50......	...... 33 00......
Live Stock "...... 28.00	...... 29 00......	...... 57 00......
Cordwood 25 p. c. over lumber rates.		
Flour, per brl...... 0 27	...... 0 28......	...... 0 55......
Grain, per bush.		
60 lbs........... 0 7½	...... 0 7½......	...... 0 15......
Goods, per ton, 3rd		
class.............. 3 80	...... 4 00......	...... 7 80......

Table of freight, *via* Central or T. G. and B. R. at the same rate of freight per mile that is charged from Collingwood to Toronto, on freight from the shores of the Georgian Bay.

Lumber (per car)..$17 50
Live Stock " 22 70
Flour (per brl.).. 0 27½
Grain (per bush. of 60 lbs.).................................. 0 8½
Goods (per ton, 3rd class)..................................... 3 53
Cordwood, lumber rates, (per cord)........................ 2 50
Staves (per car)... 17 50

The Northern Railway Company profess to carry cordwood at 25 per ct. over lumber rates, which exorbitant charge, combined with the difficulties and obstructions placed in the way of trade in cordwood, amount to a practical prohibition, which can be seen from the following copy of a notice posted in all the Northern Railroad stations:—

"NORTHERN RAILWAY OF CANADA—CORDWOOD.

" Notice is herby given, that in future NO CORDWOOD WILL " BE RECEIVED, OR ALLOWED TO BE STACKED AT THE STATIONS, " OR ON THE SIDE OF THE TRACK, EXCEPTING only such as IS " SOLD and delivered *under contract to the Company;* nor will " any cordwood be hereafter carried except from Regular Sta-

" tions, nor then except when *loaded from the teams direct* on " the cars.

" All Train Rates and Special Contracts are hereby cancelled.

" FRED. CUMBERLAND,
" Managing Director.

" N. R. C. OFFICE, }
" Toronto, 15th May, 1866." }

How far these obstructive [conditions are calculated by the Company to protect or cheapen the cost of fuel to themselves, or to promote the interests represented by the following peculiar letter it may be difficult to determine.

{ " NORTHERN RAILWAY OF CANADA,
" ENGINEER'S OFFICE,
" TORONTO, December 27th, 1866.

" DEAR SIR,—The Northern Railway Company have about " four thousand cords of dry wood to dispose of—the greater " part of which will be between Lefroy and Allandale. There " will probably be about 1,000 cords north of Allandale. Be- " low I give rates per train of twelve cars each, for one day's " service, inclusive of loading, each car to carry not more than " 6½ cords:—

Bradford and all South..............................$185 per train.
North of Bradford, and including Lefroy......... 195   "
North of Lefroy, and including Allandale........ 215   "
North of Allandale................................,.......... 225   "

" If you wish to make an offer for this wood, please state in " writing the rate per cord you are willing to give on the line " of Railway. You may either say one price all round; or, " if you prefer it, name a price up to each station, varying in " proportion to our train rates. I wish you to give a reply by " bearer, as I am anxious to close the matter this P.M.

" The Company will probably run two wood trains, in order " to have it all down before the timber business commences, " which will be about the middle of February.

" Each train load to be paid for in cash as it is delivered in " Toronto. *The wood will be allowed to remain a reasonable time* " *in the Company's yard in Toronto, in order to afford the pur-* " *chaser a fair opportunity of hauling it away.*

" I remain, yours truly,

" G. W. MOBERLY,
" Per J. H. J."

The promoters of the Toronto, Grey and Bruce and Toronto and Nipissing Railways, ¡desiring to disarm the future executive officers of these companies of such dangerous power, and wishing to put the questions of cordwood and foreign traffic on an equitable basis, beyond the power of interference by future Boards of Directors or General Managers, propose to insert stringent clauses in their charters to protect the public interests on these important points (see copies of applications for charters.)

In considering the foregoing statements and tables, you will see that trade is diverted from its natural channel and markets by the irresponsible and arbitrary fiats of gentlemen who necessarily· study and carry out a policy favourable to the interests of their English employers, however disadvantageous .that policy may be to the interests of the districts affected, or damaging to the prosperity of the capital of this Province. One-fifth of the rolling stock now employed in carrying to the eastern termini of the G. T. R., would bring to this city from the western section G. T. R., at fair rates, all the produce, timber, cordwood, &c., destined for consumption in this or intermediate markets. If other sections of the G. T. R. fail to pay expenses, is it our fault that we have to make good the loss?

The G. T. R. Company like to load their cars at the western termini and run them through at round freights to the other termini—Quebec or Portland—and re-load for the same journey backwards, which may be for the advantage of the Company, although this is doubtful, but is very far from being for the true interests of the farmers west of Toronto, which is the main point for our consideration.

Only *one-tenth* of the wheat and flour of Upper Canada were marketed in Montreal last year, which is a startling fact. They will not buy our fall wheat. It has all to be sold to Americans, and the G. T. R. carries no fall wheat except the insignificant portion shipped for consumption in Maine and Boston. The whole of our fall wheat, and the greater portion of our fall wheat flour, and all our barley, have to be shipped across Lake Ontario, as our best markets for these articles are along the Erie canal, in the rich towns accessible therefrom, and in the great city of New York. Buffalo also receives for distribution a small portion of our produce, when western stuff is deficient in quality or quantity.

Mr. Hatch says: "In the New World the chief effort of statesmanship, applied to material objects, is to develop as early and to as great an extent as is possible the resources of our own territories. Other nations are compelled to seek abroad for those means of employment and prosperity which we possess at home, and to an extent practically unlimited. This development is the chief object of our wisest political economy; and it can in no other way be so well promoted as by constructing or enlarging the various means of communication which carry emigrants to those regions where their toil will be most amply rewarded, and at the same time bring the productions of all parts of our common country to those markets where they command the highest price, or, in other words, return the greatest remuneration to human labour. We thus also stimulate immigration from abroad, and provide the essential elements for the most profitable foreign trade.

"Commerce has always, in every country, sought first the channels formed by nature, as the easiest and cheapest highways from the interior to the seaboard."

Our Local Parliament will have no more important duty to consider than how to encourage the construction and extension of the means of communication, which will *carry out the trees and carry in the people* to those places where their toil will reward their employers, and provide themselves with means, in a few years, to employ those whom they will invite by their prosperity to join them.

Our immigration business drags somehow. Of the few who come determined to settle in Canada, a portion re-emigrate to the States; mainly because they cannot afford to buy dear wild land, and are afraid to "tackle the trees," burn them, and have to wait two years before they can eat bread of their own growing. The construction of cheap railways, *bound by law to carry cordwood*, would in many instances remove those difficulties; therefore these roads ought to be built, and pushed into the heart of the country, and the labourers would form the nucleus of settlements, wherever settlements were possible on the route to Nipissing.

It is unnecessary to enlarge on the general increase of material wealth to be derived from the construction of railways on a basis of sound engineering and commercial principles, to connect Bruce, Grey, Victoria and Ontario, and the large fertile intervening tract of country, with this city, and through it, with all the rich and important cities of New York and neighbouring States, containing a population of twelve millions of people, who are our natural and indispensable customers for our choicest productions, and who will continue to be so, notwithstanding their present erratic legislation.

It can be clearly seen how the general interests *are to be advanced* by stations becoming market towns, and how idle water privileges will become, under the stimulus of railway traffic, busy centres of manufacturing industry. Household comforts, now beyond the reach of many, will be easily attainable in exchange for all minor farm produce, wood, &c.

There is a difficulty in getting new railroads, because the waste, extravagance and mismanagement attending the construction of our present lines have rendered them unprofitable. The money spent in their construction, so far as the first shareholders are concerned, has been *totally lost*, except in the case of the Great Western Railway. The system of paying contractors their own exorbitant prices, if they took stock in part payment, was ruinous. In consequence of this untoward state of matters, not a dollar can be borrowed to construct much needed lines on the most thoroughly economical principles, without some more tangible basis than mere Canada Railroad Stocks.

It is contrary to the genius of our Government to guarantee the interest on outlays for purely local works; therefore, sufficient land must be obtained from the Local Government to induce capitalists, or men with any spare means in Canada and elsewhere, to take the requisite amount of stock in these roads to secure their immediate construction.

If every $100 stock carried with it a patent or scrip for a *certain lot* of 100 acres of land, and if these bonds and the land scrip were saleable and transferable, separately or together, the amount of money required to build cheap, light, Narrow-Guage Railways, would very quickly be forthcoming, and the scream of the locomotive would very soon awaken the echoes of our solitudes, and startle our interior population into sudden activity and prosperity; *and ourselves would largely benefit from the credit derived from land, which, under present circumstances, not one in one thousand of our people of the present generation will ever see.* The land referred to is east of the Georgian Bay Canal, north of the new townships, all the way to and beyond lake Nipissing, to which the people of Toronto propose in time to extend the line projected to Gull River.

Who are so well entitled to the use of the Crown Lands, as a basis of credit for promoting important and necessary public works, as the very men by whose hardships, toil and industry these lands have been rendered or are likely to be made of any practical value, and who are the parties mainly to be benefited by the construction of these railroads?

It would be highly impolitic, in view of the progress desired for the country, as well as cruel to these less favoured settlers, to deny them the advantages obtained at such enormous and unnecessary cost, by those who live in more favoured localities.

The land will not be *removed*, and these roads, for which a small portion of it is sold, will be the very means of filling it with immigrants.

The Government sold last year, in the County of Simcoe, 300,000 or 400,000 acres of land, at public auction at Barrie, at prices varying from 10c. to 20c. an acre; what, therefore, is the worth of the unbroken wilderness round lake Nipissing?—*Not a farthing*, unless we point a railroad in that direction, *which cannot be done* without direct assistance from the Government, or by the aid of a land grant. The Grand Trunk style of railroad, and cost, is beyond our power under any circumstances. Therefore we must seek the establishment of a system of railways more suitable to our means and requirements, as has been successfully done in Australia, India, Norway and Sweeden.

As much as possible of the stocks of these two new railways, one to run north-west and the other north-east of this city, should be taken by the people of the country traversed and the people of Toronto, so as to secure local management and proper attention to local interests.

The success of these sort of Railways is not problematical, it is an ascertained fact, proven by years of experience. Our Railroad managers, through their engineers and otherwise, may attack the system proposed on the Central Route, by a new company, as a means of defeating the building *of any railway* on this route; but with active and energetic co-operation, these roads will be built, as they are favoured and promoted by the most wealthy and influential citizens, who lack neither skill, means, nor energy, to secure for farmers and the citizens of Toronto the benefits of *a direct road bound to carry cordwood* from these vast counties.

Mr. Fowler's scheme did not interest the citizens of Toronto, because they *knew* the money for such a road could not be obtained, and he was easily overpowered by Mr. Cumberland's Northern Railway friends and the apathy of the supporters of the Central Route, although *numbering all other citizens* excepting those who were afraid the Central Route might connect with the G. T. R. at a point west of this city. The parties now interested have no such fears; nor have they any view to big contracts, for their personal gain, which may have influenced public opinion as to Mr. Fowler's programme, as well as that of the promoters of the Durham Branch. The adoption of a system of small contracts, in building new roads, is *sure* protection from the depredations of large contractors, who despise such two-penny half-penny ways of doing business.

Contracts, so small as to be within the reach of local contractors, are the essence of cheap railway making.

The merchants of Toronto, the nature of whose business teaches them to understand the routes of traffic best calculated to promote the prosperity of Toronto and the country, are thoroughly alive to the necessity of preventing the very sources of their trade from being dried up by the formation of lines of railroad to connect with second-rate markets, objectionable and expensive harbours, or with railroads the policy of which is inimical to the true interests of the country and of this city.

No effort should be spared to secure for this city her just share of the trade of the interior, and the benefit of being the terminus for two such promising lines of railroad, either of which will bring more farm or forest produce to this market than any of the other three. Along the routes of the new lines our merchants would find their business increase three or five-fold. Our workshops, warehouses and vessels, would be taxed to the limits of their capacity, in supplying facilities for the new business which these roads would pour into the city. Property would increase in value, not by reason of undue speculation, but on account of the competition for premises to accommodate an increasing and busy population. Taxes would be lightened in proportion as the number and means increased of those from whom they were to be collected.

A railway which terminates at a point on another railway becomes subsidiary to the trunk line, and the branch is at all times liable, from change of management or policy, to be victimized, even to the rejection of its business, until it come to the terms of the main line. Examples of this nature occurred recently in Ireland.

In considering the advantages of Toronto, as the best market and shipping port for the products of the country, consequently the best terminus for the Railways through Grey and Bruce, Ontario and Victoria, it should not be forgotten that Toronto is now the seat of our Local Government—as well as the financial, legal and educational capital of Ontario.

A great deal of business will therefore be transacted here, involving a large concentration of travel from the interior on the city, which should be had in view in discussing the merits of the various routes, as the people of the interior, for the present and future generations, will not like to "box the compass" before getting to the capital city.

The annexed petitions are being circulated for signature, on the routes of the Toronto, Grey and Bruce, and Toronto and Nipissing Railways, and it is hoped by the Provisional Directors of the two Companies that energetic efforts will be made by all concerned, to assist in every way possible, and combine their resources, with a view to the *active prosecution of work on these railroads next summer.*

To the Honorable the Legislative Assembly of the Province of Ontario, in Parliament assembled.

THE PETITION OF THE UNDERSIGNED RATEPAYERS OF THE COUNTIES OF YORK, ONTARIO AND VICTORIA.

HUMBLY SHEWETH:

That the large tract of Country lying between the City of Toronto and Lake Nipissing is without any means of communication or of Transport, except such as is afforded by the common roads of the country.

That, in the judgment of your Petitioners, the construction of Railroad through that section of country would materially aid its settlement, and the development of its resources.

Wherefore, your Petitioners humbly pray your Honorable Body, that a charter may be granted for a Railway from Toronto to Lake Nipissing, traversing the counties of York, Ontario, and Victoria; and that said charter contain a clause binding the said railway to carry cordwood, or any wood for fuel, at a rate not to exceed two-and-a-half cents per mile per cord, for all stations exceeding fifty miles, and at a rate not exceeding three cents per cord per mile for all stations under fifty miles.

And your Petitioners, as in duty bound, will ever pray.

To the Honorable the Legislative Assembly of the Province of Ontario, in Parliament assembled.

THE PETITION OF THE UNDERSIGNED RATEPAYERS OF THE COUNTIES OF YORK, ONTARIO AND VICTORIA.

HUMBLY SHEWETH: .

That, in the opinion of your Petitioners, a Railway, running between the City of Toronto and Lake Nipissing, is required to open up that section of country, rich in undeveloped resources, and that its construction would contribute in a large degree to the resources of the Province.

That whereas the people residing in the Counties of York, Ontario and Victoria, in those sections through which the Railway would run, have borne their share of the burdens imposed on the country in providing Railway accommodation for the people on the lines of the Grand Trunk and other Railways, your Petitioners are of opinion that the people of the said section have an undeniable, just and equitable claim on the Province for a Grant of Public Lands, to enable them to construct the said Railroad, to open up the country and afford to settlers in the interior access to the markets.

Your Petitioners, therefore, humbly pray that so much of the Public Lands as, in the estimation of your Honorable House, will meet the necessities and requirements of the said Toronto and Nipissing Railroad, may be set apart for that purpose, and such steps taken as will lead to the successful completion of this most important undertaking.

And your Petitioners, as in duty bound, will ever pray.

Toronto, this   day of   , 1867.

PETITION FOR CHARTER FOR THE TORONTO, GREY AND BRUCE RAILWAY.

To the Honorable the Legislative Assembly of the Province of Ontario, in Parliament assembled.

THE PETITION OF THE UNDERSIGNED RATEPAYERS OF THE COUNTIES OF YORK, CARDWELL, WELLINGTON, GREY AND BRUCE,

HUMBLY SHEWETH:

That, in the opinion of your Petitioners, a Railway, running between the City of Toronto and a point on Lake Huron, in the County of Bruce (said point to be determined by the County Council of Bruce) with a branch to Owen Sound from Mount Forest, Durham, or a point east of them, through the County of Grey, is necessary to open up that extensive and fertile portion of the country, which is without Railway accommodation, or other means of rapid development. The greater number of your Petitioners residing forty miles from Railway Markets, the market towns on Lake Huron, west and north of the Counties of Bruce and Grey, are, during five months of the year, cut off from the export trade, while the want of access to large centres of consumption in winter militates against the value of many articles, the produce of our farms and forests.

That, in the judgment of your Petitioners, the construction of a Railway through that section of country is indispensable to the inhabitants of 4,300 square miles of a rich and only partially settled agricultural country, the prosperity of which would largely contribute to the power and revenue of the Dominion, by increasing the population, the exports and imports, and by sustaining local, financial and industrial establishments.

Wherefore your commissioners humbly pray your Honorable Body that a Charter may be granted for a Railway from Toronto to Mount Forest or Durham, thence to a point on Lake Huron, in the County of Bruce, with a Branch from a point on the main line north to Owen Sound, through the Counties of York, Cardwell, Wellington, Bruce and Grey; and that said Charter contain a clause binding the Railway Company to carry cordwood, or any wood for fuel, at a rate not to exceed two and one-half cents per mile per cord for all stations exceeding fifty miles, and at a rate not exceeding three cents per cord per mile for all stations under fifty miles.

That the Charter contain a clause providing that no foreign freight shall be carried at a less rate per mile for equal distances than the productions of our own country.

And your Petitioners, as in duty bound, will ever pray, &c.

PETITION FOR A LAND GRANT, TO ASSIST IN THE CONSTRUCTION OF THE T. G. & B. RAILWAY.

To the Honorable the Legislative Assembly of the Province of Canada, in Parliament Assembled.

THE PETITION OF THE UNDERSIGNED RATEPAYERS OF THE COUNTIES OF YORK, CARDWELL, WELLINGTON, GREY AND BRUCE,

HUMBLY SHEWETH:

That, in the opinion of your Petitioners, a Railway running from Toronto to or near Orangeville, thence to or near Mount Forest, both in the County of Wellington, thence to or near Walkerton, in the County of Bruce, thence to a point on Lake Huron to be determined by the County Council of Bruce, with a Branch, from Mount Forest, or a point east of it, to Owen Sound, is necessary to the prosperity of that extensive and fertile region.

That whereas the area of the country south of the Grand Trunk and Goderich line is 9,200 square miles, with about 745 miles of existing Railways, the area of the country between the Grand Trunk and Goderich line and the Northern Railroad is 6,800 miles, of which, after leaving 2,450 miles as naturally and equitably tributary to existing lines, there remain 4,350 square miles of the richest and most fertile lands in Canada only partially settled, to be provided with the indispensable facilities of Railway communication to the existing Trunk lines, to foreign markets, and to Toronto, as the capital and commercial emporium of the Province of Ontario.

That whereas the people residing in the Counties of York, Cardwell, Wellington, Grey and Bruce, in those sections through which the said Railway would run, have borne their share of the burdens imposed on the country in providing Railway accommodation for the people in the neighbourhood of the Grand Trunk, Great Western and Northern Railways, your Petitioners are of opinion that the people of the aforesaid sections have a just and equitable claim on the Province for pecuniary assistance, or a grant of public lands, to enable the T. G. & B. Railway Co. to construct the said Railway, to open up the country.

Your Petitioners, therefore, humbly pray that so much of the idle public lands as in the estimation of your honorable House will meet the requirements or necessities of the Toronto, Grey and Bruce Railway Company, and enable them to construct a Railway on the route aforementioned, be set apart for that purpose, and such measures adopted as in the opinion of your honorable House will lead to the successful completion of this most important undertaking.

And your Petitioners, as in duty bound, will ever pray.

THE LAND QUESTION.

The projectors of these two new lines of Railway would prefer direct pecuniary aid to their enterprises from the local Government, but recognising the difficulties in the way of receiving such assistance under the existing revenue system of Ontario, *notwithstanding the justice of their claim for the people,* they prefer to join with them in soliciting a judicious apportionment of the wild lands, because a grant of a portion of them will not increase the taxation of the people of the Dominion one farthing, while the construction of these two railroads will lead in time of peace to a great increase of population and revenue and, in time of war, be of great strategic importance.

It is not inconsistent with the "free grant system" to give lands to aid in constructing these Railroads, as their advocates feel convinced that no free grants *will be taken up* between the Georgian Bay and the Ottawa, the *only place where free grants can be given* this side of Lake Nipissing and the French River, unless railroad facilities are afforded to that territory, which is nearly 200 miles square. *Alternate sections* only are desired, to a moderate extent, at or near the line of the Toronto and Nipissing Railway, and as the Government will own *the other alternate sections, to donate as free grants to actual settlers, besides the immense territory outside the railroad grants,* it follows that the stockholders of the Railroads must necessarily sell their grants cheap, or settle on the lands themselves, which would frequently be the case no doubt, as the sons of our frontier farmers would probably, in large numbers, take railroad stock with the quota of land conjoined, and go back at once to found homesteads for themselves near, or perhaps a long stride in advance of the Railroad, while nothing can induce young men to go to such uncongenial wilds under present circumstances.

It is very probable that farmers, mechanics and laborers, would really to a large extent become the proprietors of these roads, as there is less inducement to speculators or capitalists to take up lands which would for a considerable time be depressed in value, in consequence of the free grant system being in active operation *all round the railroad grants.*

It will be the duty of the Government to see, if real settlers desire these railroad stocks with land certificates attached, that a clause in the charter will prevent large capitalists from taking an undue share of stock and land until the settlers' demand is thoroughly supplied—after which it is to be hoped capitalists will lend on the stocks, or buy them to an extent sufficient to secure the construction of these works, of such exceeding consequence to the whole population of the Dominion of Canada.

We need not invite immigrants to such lands; *they will neither buy them, nor take them free,* with the condition of being ostracised from civilization, but will continue to prefer homes in the lands of the United States at $1¼ to $5 per acre on the lines of Railway which, with the assistance of very liberal land grants, are being built far in advance of settlements, towards the Rocky Mountains, into the hunting grounds of the Indians. The following extracts will show the spirit that animates those enterprising and energetic people of the far west, the bulk of them immigrants only recently emancipated from the depressing influences of poverty, who emigrate to the Great West to possess and inherit the land, and who consider the most direct route to the Capital should receive the greatest encouragement from the people of the interior, when laying down the permanent ways for their future trade.   The people of Eldon know very well on what side their bread is buttered, and understand and believe in the honest, straightforward effort, on sound business principles, by the citizens of Toronto, to get railroad communication with them, while they cannot forget the long years of false promises, and now justly suspect the new-born zeal of the *three proprietors* of the P. H. & L. R. to be only a pawn moved to checkmate the royal road to Toronto.   Let the "triumvirate" of the Lindsay Road begin their good works at home, and supply people with cars at reasonable rates, and carry cordwood at the same rate as lumber, and they may do well enough without the proposed absurd extension of their dilapidated Railroad to Beaverton and the saw mills on the Severn, which is either a crafty or unscrupulous device of the *three proprietors of the* P. H. & L. R., to tap the trade the Northern has from Lake Simcoe, and cut off the resources of its supply of pine from the Severn and Black River, or what is more likely, an attempt to continue the delusion of fifteen years' standing, that the P. H. & L. R. Co. are going to *build* an extension to Beaverton, and so frustrate the construction of the Toronto and Nipissing Railway, by enticing the people of the Townships of Eldon and Thorah to sustain the Lindsay, and withdraw their support from the road to Toronto.

The support of these Townships to the Toronto and Nipissing Railway is absolutely necessary to its construction, hence the Jesuitical arguments of its opponents.   It makes no difference to Eldon and Thorah how long or short the Toronto road will be, as they will not be called upon for more aid than *their proportion* per mile, should the road reach even to the waters of the Muskoka *the second year*.

The Toronto and Nipissing Railroad (as stated once before) was not projected to rob the Port Hope and Lindsay Railroad Company of their business, but to increase the population, the value of the land, and its products, and the area of settled, or partially settled, territory to the north-east, the unbounded prosperity of which, with railroad facilities to Toronto, would treble the business of our importers and exporters, while our banks, insurances offices, workshops, warehouses and vessels, would be taxed to the limits of their capacity in supplying facilities for the new business which would pour into this City. Property would increase in value on account of the competition for shops and dwellings to accommodate a thriving and busy population.   Taxes would be lightened in proportion as the number and means of citizens were increased.

Trusting that the people of Eldon, Thorah, and the other Townships, as well as the citizens of Toronto, will be impressed with the beneficial results to accrue from railroad intercommunication, and that they will co-operate with energy in making up for any short-comings of the promoters, and cordially assist with active vigour all efforts calculated to accomplish the immediate construction of the Toronto and Nipissing Railroad,

I remain, Sir,

Your obedient servant,

G. LAIDLAW.

Toronto, Dec. 10.

" and, in some instances, going ahead of them, causing the
" music of busy life to be heard on those beautiful prairies,
" where only yesterday silence and solitude reigned, save only
" as they were broken by the cry of the savage or the wolf, or
" the impetuous rush of herds of buffaloes, and he will have
" some conception of what is now meant by the March of
" Empire."

While the Americans are driving parallel lines of Railways
with unexampled energy and rapidity westward over their
beautiful praries, and through fertile valleys, to connect with
that on the Atlantic the civilization on the Pacific, scarcely
yet the age of a school-boy, and bind the remote ends of their
country together by chains of successive prosperous settlements, resembling nationalities—the backbone and marrow of
which are our fellow-Britons—the people of Canada must
be content to advance more slowly, north, as well as west-
wards, through a more rugged, but not less valuable territory,
of illimitable forests of magnificent timber, a vast mineral
region of ascertained wealth, and a boundless extent of rich
fertile soil, equal if not superior, *two hundred miles north of
Lake Nippising*, to that which fills the granaries of the Baltic
with the choicest cereals. This is the character of the
splendid heritage over which it is our duty and interest to
direct the march of our more conservative civilization, if not
with such gigantic strides as our neighbors, at least with a
steady and prudent progress, which will take away from us
the reproach of being unequal to our destiny.

The Government of Ontario might, with advantage to the
people, and credit to themselves, adopt the Norwegian and
Queensland system of building light narrow gauge Railroads,
upon the American policy of having the *Railroad precede the
immigrant, as a certain means of securing immediate and extensive settlement on our own magnificent public domain*,
the cost of the Railroads to be a first charge on the new
municipalities, which would undoubtedly spring up in the
vicinity of the roads with hitherto unwonted rapidity.

5

based upon our experience in other countries, and upon surveys of the intended route, and the figures are as follows :—

COST PER MILE, 5 FEET 6 INCH GAUGE.

Land and land damage, clearing and fencing............	$1,250 00
Superstructure, including allowance for sidings.........	8,800 00
Gradings, masonry, bridging and culverts, road and farm crossings, &c....................................	5,500 00
Buildings of all kinds..	1,000 00
Rolling Stock..	3,000 00
Engineering, management, and contingencies...........	3,000 00
	$22,550 00

COST PER MILE, 3 FEET 6 INCH GAUGE.

Land and land damage, clearing and fencing............	$1,150 00
Superstructure, including allowance for sidings.........	5,500 00
Grading, masonry, bridging and culverts, road and farm crossings, &c....................................	3,300 00
Buildings...	1,000 00
Rolling Stock..	2,000 00
Engineering, management, and contingencies...........	2,100 00
	$15,050 00

Showing the cost of the Narrow-gauge to be $15,050 00 per mile ; and of the Broad-gauge, $22,550 00 per mile, or an excess of 50 per cent. over the cost of the other road.

In each case the rolling stock and stations are estimated for a traffic at least equal to that now carried by the Northern Railway.

Mr. Shanly goes into a long argument to prove the truism, that "the greater the net load carried on one train by one engine, the less the cost per ton." We cannot understand in what way this bears upon the question at issue. It appears to be based upon the misconception that the weight of the Locomotives upon the Narrow-gauge is limited. The fact is, that as heavy trains can be worked with advantage upon the Narrow-gauge as upon the Broad. Mr. Shanly says that the heavier style of engine, calculated to draw larger loads, does not seem to be generally used on the Narrow-gauge lines. We would therefore state that engines of upwards of thirty-five tons weight are now being constantly used on these lines in Queensland.

As the estimate of the increased cost of the Rolling Stock is based upon this misconception, it falls to the ground, the fact being, as we can testify, that from its being lighter, the Rolling Stock on the Narrow-gauge is less costly than that on the Wide-gauge, of equal capacity.

Apart from the fact that the Count de Pamboure, referred to by Mr. Shanly, is a somewhat antiquated authority, the sad experience of the Great Western Railway of England, which is 7.0 gauge, certainly disproves his conclusion that " an engine cn that gauge will do three times as much work with less fuel as on the 4.8½ gauge." If this be so, it is a remarkable fact that Sir Daniel Gooch, now Chairman, and for many years Locomotive Superintendent of that Company, should have declared himself so strongly in favour of the narrower gauge, which is now being laid down on that Railway.

With reference to the question of transhipment, as we have ascertained that fully nine-tenths of the produce coming from the interior must, in any case, be transhipped and go forward by water, we quite agree with Mr. Shanly that *this is a matter of small importance;* and even in the case of Through Passengers and Freight, we coincide with the opinion of Captain Tyler, as expressed in page 29 of his Report to the Grand Trunk Railway, viz. : "*That with some classes of freight it is a very simple and cheap operation; and it is in fact only with regard to a small proportion of the whole traffic that it is necessary, or even desirable, to make some arrangement by which transhipment or break of bulk shall be avoided.*'

With regard to Mr. Shanly's fears that the estimate of $15,000 will be found lamentably insufficient, we have only to state that our estimates are based upon actual surveys. We do not state what we think, but what we know.

We have the honour to be,
Your obedient servants,
CHARLES DOUGLAS FOX, M.I.C.E.,
Of the Firm of Sir Charles Fox & Sons.
JOHN EDWARD BOYD, M.I.C.E.,
Engineer-in-Chief to the Government of New Brunswick.

NARROW GAUGE RAILWAY.

Mr. Fox has published the following letter in reply to one published by Mr. Reid.

SIR,—My attention has been directed to a letter from Mr. George Lowe Reid, on this subject, and although I am very unwilling to weary your readers with any further remarks upon this question, already so fully debated, I feel, in justice to myself, I must ask you to insert a few words in reply.

There is no one in the Dominion for whose professional opinion I entertain a greater respect than Mr. Reid; at the same time, that gentleman has had no experience in either the construction or working of such Narrow-gauge Railways as those in question, and no doubt feels the same prejudice against them as I myself entertained, until after careful examination of them in actual working. My firm have now been for several years constantly engaged as engineers, in the supervision of their construction in various countries, and I am therefore enabled to speak from practical experience of the results obtainable from them.

Mr. Reid gives a comparative estimate of a Broad-guage line as compared with a light Narrow-gauge line, and shows a difference of only 7½ per cent. This estimate, almost every item of which I can disprove, is admitted to be not based upon any survey of the actual country through which the railways I have the honor to represent will pass. Now, being in possession of careful surveys of a considerable portion of these railways, and having taken out the detailed quantities, I am enabled again to repeat what I have before stated, that taking the same prices and providing for the same amount of traffic in each case, a narrow-gauge light railway will cost an average of $15,000, whilst the broad-gauge light railway can not be completed for less than $20,000 a mile, an increase of 33 per cent. The details of this comparison I clearly proved under cross-examination before the committee. The Narrow-gauge railway proposed would be of the best materials in every respect, capable at once of a traffic of 300,000 tons of freight, and 200,000 passengers, and of a speed of 20 to 25 miles an hour, suited in every way to the climate of this country, and as readily cleared of snow as the broad-gauge lines. In these latter respects, we have an excellent guide in Norway, where the climate is more severe, and the drifting heavier than in Canada.

Without going into a lengthened argument upon the remainder of Mr. Reid's letter, which is based upon the same misconception which I pointed out to the committee, as to the power of the locomotives which can be employed upon the narrow-gauge railways, I would simply state the following facts, derived from actual and extensive experience, which I am at any time thoroughly prepared to substantiate :—

1st. That 12 ft. 6 in. for embankments and 13 ft. for cuttings are an ample width for the 3 ft. 6 in. gauge. These are the widths adopted in the severe climate of Norway, and have answered admirably.

2nd. That the cost of Rolling Stock, of equal capacity, is as nearly as possible the same on both gauges.

3rd. That a narrow-gauge engine can draw as much as a broad-gauge engine of the same weight, and locomotives weighing 36 tons can, if required, be used on the narrow-gauge, as they are in Australia at the present time These engines, recommended by Captain Tyler for the Grand Trunk Railway, are found to be very economical in working, and well adapted for sharp curves and frozen roads.

4th. That, as follows from the last statement, only the same number of engines are required for the same traffic on either gauge.

5th. That, as proved in India and elsewhere, the working expenses of a narrow-gauge railway, where there is a fair amount of traffic, are 65 per cent. of the receipts. With a large traffic the proportion is much reduced.

6th. That the cost of haulage on the two gauges is the same, the cost of maintaining the works less on the narrow than on the broad-gauge.

2

Lightning Source UK Ltd.
Milton Keynes UK
02 September 2010

159317UK00004BA/2/P